A Quaker Reading of Mark's Gospel

A Quaker Reading of Mark's Gospel

To See the Invisible

PATRICIA DALLMANN

RESOURCE *Publications* • Eugene, Oregon

A QUAKER READING OF MARK'S GOSPEL
To See the Invisible

Copyright © 2025 Patricia Dallmann. All rights reserved. Except for brief quotations in critical publications or reviews, no part of this book may be reproduced in any manner without prior written permission from the publisher. Write: Permissions, Wipf and Stock Publishers, 199 W. 8th Ave., Suite 3, Eugene, OR 97401.

Resource Publications
An Imprint of Wipf and Stock Publishers
199 W. 8th Ave., Suite 3
Eugene, OR 97401

www.wipfandstock.com

PAPERBACK ISBN: 979-8-3852-5145-2
HARDCOVER ISBN: 979-8-3852-5146-9
EBOOK ISBN: 979-8-3852-5147-6

06/19/25

Scripture is quoted from the King James Version of the Bible, copyright 1990 by Thomas Nelson Publishers.

Scripture is quoted from the New English Bible, copyright 1971 by Cambridge University Press and Oxford University Press.

And as the light opens and exerciseth thy conscience, it will open to thee parables and figures, and it will let thee see invisible things, which are clearly seen by that which is invisible in thee.... [T]hat which is invisible is the light within thee, which he who is invisible hath given thee a measure of.

—George Fox

Contents

Introduction to the Gospel (Mark 1) | 1
Faith in Life Itself (2:1–12) | 7
Lord of the Sabbath (2:13–28) | 13
Beyond Idealism (3:1–6) | 20
On Unity (3:20–35) | 23
On Parables (4:1–34) | 28
The Other Side (4:33–41) | 34
The First Workings of the Lord (5:1–20) | 37
A Want of God (5:21–43) | 42
Gospel Work (Mark 6) | 49
The Prophet Schooled (Mark 7) | 57
Our Example (Mark 8) | 62
Preparing the Disciples (Mark 9) | 70
Meaning in Life (Mark 10) | 76
The Subsidiary Flesh (Mark 11) | 83
The Lesson of the Fig Tree (11:12–14, 20–22) | 91
The Practice of Religion (Mark 12) | 93
Right Use of Our Tradition (12:18–34) | 101
You Shall Read Your Figures (Mark 13) | 107
The Way Shown (Mark 14) | 116
Seeing It Through (Mark 15) | 122
Taking In and Giving Out (Mark 16) | 128
Bibliography | 135

Introduction to the Gospel (Mark 1)

The beginning of the gospel of Jesus Christ, the Son of God; As it is written in the prophets, Behold, I send my messenger before thy face, which shall prepare thy way before thee. The voice of one crying in the wilderness, prepare ye the way of the Lord, make his paths straight (1–3).

HUMANITY CARRIES GIFTS GIVEN to no other creature, yet we have not been given the power to justify our existence. The gospel, which is the power of God,[1] supplies this necessity so that we may give over faulty, fallen attempts to self-justify and at last rest assured in the faith that makes us whole. In this gospel power, we feel complete: Truth's perfection is known; our ancient yearning is met and satisfied. In the first chapter of Mark, whose topic is "the beginning of the gospel of Jesus Christ," the way is introduced.

As in much of Scripture, the text here brings types and figures of spiritual conditions and processes into view, so we can more easily recognize and name inward truths that otherwise might remain hidden and obscure. The text does provide

---

1. Epigraph. Mark 1:1–3 (The King James Version [KJV] is used throughout the essay). "The gospel is the power of God which turns against that which bondageth, to wit, the corruptions, and so gives liberty and freedom to the captives; and this, which is the power of God, is glad tidings . . . that which gives liberty and freedom to all, is glad tidings" (Fox, *Works*, 3:442).

historical and geographical information, but such objective facts lack spiritual significance if not related to inward realities. The Bible and early Friends writings are texts about humanity's spiritual malaise and its return to vigor; to view these spiritual resources primarily as fields in which scholars harvest ideas to increase our store of knowledge is to disregard the value and purpose of the writings. Since the 1990s, spiritual exposition of biblical and Friends writings has been largely co-opted by a scholarly focus upon the context provided by historical events, philosophies, and languages, which has kept pace with our society's veering toward the materialism of technology. Should Friends return to gospel order, the present time, in hindsight, likely will be seen as a period in which scholarly pursuit stood in place of prophetic faith, and information pinch-hit for wisdom. Friends knew "that being bred at Oxford and Cambridge was not enough to fit and qualify men to be ministers of Christ."[2] Yet in their time and in ours, the loss of the gospel allows scholarly information to step into the void. Early Friends were adept at drawing parallels between the events and people in Scripture and inward, spiritual life because they had traveled the complete path to salvation. That inward journey opened Scripture's imagery for them ("they could see invisible things . . . by that which is invisible[3]) and using that imagery, they were enabled to record and communicate their experiential discovery of Christ Within, a discovery they knew to have universal significance, beyond information that is intellectually gathered, dispersed, and received.

In the following paragraph, early Friend Margaret Fell provides an example of writing that offers spiritual wisdom about the human condition. She correlates the messenger-prophets referred to in the first chapter of Mark—those who prepare the way of the Lord—to the "measure of the Substance" present within each person.

---

2. Fox, *Works*, 1:71.
3. Fox, *Works*, 4:34.

Introduction to the Gospel (Mark 1)

So a measure of the Substance, and of the life of all the types and figures, thou hast in thee, if thou be faithful and obedient when it checks and calls thee to repentance. For the baptism of repentance, which washeth away the filth of the flesh, thou art not yet come to: no, nor the first principle that leads to it, which is the messenger that goes before him to prepare the way for him which baptized with the Holy Ghost and with fire.[4]

As do the outward messenger-prophets in Scripture,[5] the inward "measure of the Substance . . . checks and calls [one] to repentance." All must first come to this measure of the Substance in themselves, as all in Judea and Jerusalem outwardly came to John, "confessing their sins" (5). Fell states this is the "first principle that leads to being "baptize[d] with the Holy Ghost," a work to be done by Jesus, says John (8): a work to be done inwardly by Christ, the Light.

Baptism indicates a new state has been entered, and John's baptism of Jesus signals his divine acceptance: "Thou art my beloved Son, in whom I am well pleased" (11). Inwardly, baptism with the Holy Ghost reveals this divine relationship. And entering into it, one "immediately" finds oneself driven by that same Spirit (12) into a solitude where there is longtime temptation (13) to become one among the many "wild beasts"[6] (12). The badgering,

---

4. Fell, *Zeal*, 58–59.

5. Verse 2 echoes Malachi 3:1a: "Behold I will send my messenger, and he shall prepare the way before me: and the Lord, whom ye seek, shall suddenly come to his temple." Verse 3 echoes Isaiah 40:3: "The voice of him that crieth in the wilderness, Prepare ye the way of the Lord, make straight in the desert a highway for our God."

6. "Some men have the nature of swine wallowing in the mire. Some have the nature of dogs, to bite both the sheep and one another. Some have the nature of lions, to tear, devour, and destroy. Some the nature of wolves, to tear and devour the lambs and sheep of Christ: and some the nature of the serpent, (that old adversary,) to sting, envenom and poison. . . . Some men have the natures of other beasts and creatures, minding nothing but earthly and visible things, and feeding without the fear of God. Some have the nature of a horse, to prance and vapour in their strength, and to be swift in doing evil. Some have the nature of tall sturdy oaks, to flourish and spread in wisdom and strength, who are strong in evil, which must perish and come to the fire." Fox, *Works*,

hounding ploys of Satan, however, cannot degrade those who attend to the support heaven offers (13).

THE BEGINNING OF JESUS'S MINISTRY (15-20)

Jesus's ministry begins with his announcement that describes the spiritual situation: "The time is fulfilled, and the kingdom of God is at hand," and it continues with instruction to his hearers to find their place within this new situation: "repent ye, and believe the gospel" (15).

His next step is to gather disciples, two sets of two brothers: Simon and Andrew, then James and John. Calling two simultaneously is a narrative device to signify Jesus has the stature to lead. If only one disciple were called at a time, the reader's attention would be diverted from Jesus to that disciple. (What was it about that particular man that made Jesus call him?) The intent here, however, is to present Jesus as the adept, rightful leader. That a second pair of brothers (James and John) is called immediately after the first pair (Simon and Andrew) simply underscores Jesus's position as leader. "Come ye after me" is his call (17).

THE NATURE OF HIS WORK (21-39)

Both beginning and ending verses of this passage provide the same information: "[Jesus] entered into the synagogue, and taught" (21), and "he preached in their synagogues" (39). Teaching and preaching are his work (38), and he does so with authority (22) because he has the gospel, the power of God, to direct his speech. In the intervening verses (23-34), however, he does other work: he heals "them that were diseased, and them that were possessed with devils" (32). That these healings are sandwiched between the beginning and ending statements that describe his work as verbal communication is to say that the Word of God, Christ, heals the

---

1:106-7.

Introduction to the Gospel (Mark 1)

soul. The outward healings in this passage figuratively manifest the inward, spiritual healing that the Inward Christ effects.

The first healing is of a man with an unclean spirit (23–26). What distinguishes this man as devil-possessed is his conscious opposition to goodness. "I know thee who thou art, the Holy One of God," he addresses Jesus. "[A]rt thou come to destroy us?" Fully aware of his own defiance, the demon is determined to continue unchallenged: "Let us alone," he pleads. His use of plural pronouns, "us" and "we," throughout indicates the presence of a divided self: he's aware of the might and right of the holy ("the measure of the Substance") within his conscience, and he rebels against it.

That Jesus commands the man to be silent ("[h]old thy peace" [25]) shows that the first step toward healing is to block the false gains afforded by the practice of evil. The demon's speaking gains him control and power, an idol frequently worshiped by the devil-possessed. Jesus's command to be silent prepares the way, makes the path straight (3–4), so the demon can be dismissed ("come out of him" [25]). Having been deprived of power, the demon has no reason to remain. This story is an example of an inward, spiritual process that is described through figurative imagery.

The second type of healing that Jesus does is simpler: it is a healing of a disease. Peter's mother-in-law "lay sick of a fever" (30). A disease differs from devil-possession in that there is nothing to be gained from being ill: one is simply unable to feel and function well; there is a loss of power, not a false gain. Jesus heals the woman by taking her hand and lifting her up (31). Unlike the devil-possessed man, she doesn't speak; there is no false assertion of power. Once healed, however, she is empowered to minister (31). There is a self-awareness in the woman; she feels her debilitated state, and thus Jesus can return her to health in a simple manner: by taking her hand, a gesture of comfort, and lifting her up (31), signifying resurrection to life.

At the end of the day, as both "the diseased and them that were possessed with devils" (32) are brought to Jesus, we understand that all humanity is in need of healing and to be found in one of the two groups described: the "diseased" figuratively representing the suffering of those who are dispirited, not knowing the Spirit of Christ; and those "possessed with devils" figuratively representing all who defy their consciences for some illicit gain. Jesus extends healing to both.

THE LEPER (40–45)

In the final passage of the chapter, both Jesus's work and social position become more complex. He is now approached by someone who has heard of his healing power and beseeches him to heal him of leprosy. The leper exhibits the salient traits found in each of the two former healings: like the devil-possessed (23, 26–27), he's said to be unclean (40–42), and like the humble woman, he shows humility in kneeling before Jesus. The combined features of the two in the one to be healed indicate the onset of the increasing complexity Jesus will be required to handle as his ministry expands.

Further complications become evident when the leper disregards Jesus's instruction to "say nothing to any man" and to honor the tradition by following its prescriptions (44). Jesus has the power to heal, but he does not control the social ramifications of his healing, and this passage foreshadows the conflict with the worldly religious hierarchy that will beset and complicate his mission.

This chapter's telling of the beginning of the gospel of Jesus Christ began with its prophetic context, revealed its origin to be divine acceptance, and intimated there are predatory temptations in a spiritually deserted world. Jesus showed himself adept as a leader, a preacher and teacher, and a healer. The chapter details a steady increase in Jesus's power and scope but concludes on an ambiguous note. His success is described in terms of limitation: he "could no more openly enter into the city but was without in desert places: and they came to him from every quarter" (45).

May we each "from every quarter" go to the inward, "desert places" where Christ and his teaching and healing are found.

Faith in Life Itself (2:1–12)

FOR THREE GENERATIONS, THE women in the Murphy family—daughters, granddaughters, and great-granddaughters—had agreed that Grandma Bessie's home was as close to earthly paradise as could be asked. Abounding with flower beds; herb and vegetable gardens, for summer bounty and winter storage; a grape arbor; raspberries; and an apple orchard, her home offered with each visit new growth, beauty, and good things to eat. Beatrice Elizabeth Murphy (Grandma Bessie to us) had filled her home and life with a wealth that was uniquely hers, such as the eighteen-inch geode that leaned against the step to the entry porch and announced her fascination with rocks and gems, a topic that filled the bookcase just inside the door. The wealth the geode intimated was not the kind recorded in bank statements but was instead the inner wealth of largesse, wisdom, and beauty, and this the geode's crystalline center aptly symbolized.

It was the abundance of the place that made it a paradise for us all. In the kitchen, the largest room in the house, was a massive wood-burning oven where all the baking had been done for decades. A hand pump stood just outside the back door, ready to bring up a cool drink of water from deep in the earth. Alongside the east-facing wall was an outdoor shower enclosed by a screen of morning glories that protected our modesty early each day. A rain barrel stood at one corner of the house, and a privy was a way down the path, past the hollyhocks. On summer mornings, there was sparkling dew on the grass and always the Zen-flute call of a mourning dove that drew forth our stillness and wonder. Throughout our childhood, my sister (three years my junior) and my aunt (two years my senior) had long summer days outside, playing endless games of imagination and croquet and taking turns on the tire swing. When twilight came with the glow of lightning bugs and the rise of the moon, there was hide-and-seek until the sky turned dark, the air cool, the stars sharp and clear, and the call was heard to come inside.

Some afternoons, though, when the heat of the Iowa summer became too much for us, we chose the indoors and would entertain ourselves with board games on the living room floor. It is here that I will introduce my great-grandfather T. Edward Murphy, Grandma Bessie's husband. My memory of him is just one thing: he sat in a rocking chair—not three feet from our game on the floor—and said nothing: not a word to us children, ever. I was but four years old when he died in 1955, but even at four, I realized his total silence was strange, and so privately in the kitchen, I asked my grandmother why he never spoke. Her answer implanted itself in my memory when she said, "He was betrayed by a friend." I don't remember her explaining more than that, but I do recall the sorrow I felt as I heard her words and realized that my grandfather had been hurt so deeply by another that he had stopped talking altogether.

I am surprised but very grateful that my grandmother answered my question honestly. I am also surprised and grateful that at an early age, I was given the intimation that the condition of one's soul dramatically affects one's life and that there is an invisible vulnerability in everyone, even grown-ups.

ONE SICK OF PALSY

Like the man "sick of the palsy" in the second chapter of Mark, my grandfather was unable to move forward with his life; he was paralyzed into silence and a rocking chair. With my grandfather, the cause of the debility was attributed directly to another: a betraying friend. While no such direct correlation is made to an offending

Faith in Life Itself (2:1-12)

party in the Mark 2 story, there are subtle indications that the man's suffering was precipitated by another.

Four of the man's friends bear him and his bed to Jesus, and they go to great lengths to see that he receives attention: they break up the roof and lower his bed (4). It is the friends' faith that Jesus sees, and, as a result of that faith, he pronounces the debilitated man's sins forgiven (5). In bringing the friends and their faith into this story (singular for a gospel healing story) and making them the precipitating factor in the healing, the point is made that we humans are social beings: sin in one can spread to sin in another; the betrayal of one can lead to the paralysis or diminishment of life in another. We are being told that fact in this story when we see the social dynamic in reverse: the faith of these four friends leads to the forgiveness of, or absence of, sin in another.

Please note that I did not say that the care and concern of these friends effected the man's recovery. In this Bible story, it is Jesus's work to discern—i.e., to judge—faith to be present and sin to be past. And the outward events of the story, as always, parallel the inward event: Jesus Christ appears within to announce that faith is present and sin is past and forgiven.

We might ask, however, wasn't it another's sin and not the paralytic's—or my grandfather's? Why is it that the victim is specified as having sin? For that is what Jesus does when he says: "Son, thy sins be forgiven thee" (5). In this world, there is and will be endless provocation and victimization,[1] but it is we ourselves who allow the sinful behavior of others to diminish our own souls. In allowing that, we take on sin ourselves, for the soul's death or diminishment is an affront to God from whom our souls are descended and by whom they are to be sustained. I say this not to shame victims but to outline the process by which we become entangled in life-diminishing social stumbling and to strengthen the soul so that it does not fall into fatal injury but finds its way clear to health and wholeness.

---

1. Epigraph. Penington, *Works*, 3:190. "Then said he unto the disciples, It is impossible but that offences will come: but woe unto him, through whom they come!" (Luke 17:1) The King James Version is used throughout this essay.

The paralyzed man in chapter 2 is a figure for the immobilized condition of the soul suffering the sickness of despair, and the friends who bear the man to Jesus are likewise a figurative allusion to the foursquare honoring of the virtue of life itself when the soul is sick. It is not any particular quality in the paralytic's life that the friends honor, for no such quality is mentioned, and the man is completely inactive and silent. Rather, the friends honor and respect the man's life for itself alone, devoid as it is of utility or advantage.

In like manner, a person must retain faith in life itself when his soul is under such extreme duress that he finds no ability to function or move forward in life. At this low, seemingly forsaken state, when there appears no way forward and no incentive in the world to carry on, it is too often the case that faith in the virtue of life is set aside, and the self yields to the demonic. That is to say, faith in life is replaced by faith in death: honoring truth and life is replaced by succumbing to spiritual death: deceit, enmity, or impurity.

In refusing the demonic entry to occupy and sinfully energize or "enliven" the soul, however, the lifeless, depleted self nobly endures without expectation or hope. Enduring unto the end is the faith required and seen by God in his Son on the cross; it is likewise required and seen by God in us as we undergo the inward cross. It is that faith—called in Quaker tradition "dying to the self"—that allows the Son of God, the Son of man, to say to us, his new brethren, "Son, thy sins be forgiven thee" (5). Risen and again moving forward, newly restored and resurrected to life from death-like despair, we are thus empowered to go our way to our true home as sons of God: "Arise, and take up thy bed, and go thy way into thine house" (11).

Faith in Life Itself (2:1–12)

THE SKILLFUL PHYSICIAN[2]

It is appropriate that this presentation of Christ's healing of the soul should open the second chapter of Mark's Gospel. We learned in the first chapter that Jesus heals both the possessed and the diseased (1:32), and immediately following in this second chapter, we've been given more detailed information on the particulars of the diseased soul and the steps needed for its restoration to health.

Just as the scribes assert their shallow apprehension of religion in the segment following Jesus's healing pronouncement, there will be those today who cling to their idea that this story should be taken at face value as the healing of a physical ailment. Jesus, according to this perspective, differs from us and wields magical, divine, healing power bestowed by God upon him alone (just as the scribes attributed the power to forgive sins to God alone [7]). Both of these faulty interpretations mistakenly presume to revere God and Jesus but instead exhibit a failure to know and understand the inward movement toward salvation that God has ordained, and Jesus taught and exemplified. This false faith rests upon doctrines that have been taught, learned, and taught again, as surely was the "faith" of the scribes: "Why doth this man thus speak blasphemies? Who can forgive sins but God only?" (7)

LIFE ITSELF

My family offered beauty, opportunity, and strong values to us children growing up, but it offered little guidance on the true path of salvation. There was no mention of my great-grandfather Murphy after he was gone—at least that I ever heard—and I assume the reason was the adults had an unspoken understanding that life had pitfalls and tragedies that were best kept hidden, ignored, and forgotten. Getting on and moving forward with life was the goal, as well as the means.

---

2. Penington writes: "Christ is the skillful Physician; he cures the disease, by removing the cause" (*Works*, 1:128).

Perhaps there will be more of us in the future who, while recognizing the goodness of a plentiful life, will yet hold to the belief in the virtue of life itself when despondency arrives to strip away our capacity to move forward. We will let faith in life itself carry us for a time, which, like the four friends in the story, will go to great lengths to bring us into the presence of Christ Within. It is there in Christ's presence that we will come to know his healing and to have bestowed upon us—at last—the gift of Life Itself.

> Beloved, think it not strange concerning the fiery trial which is to try you, as though some strange thing happened unto you: But rejoice, inasmuch as ye are partakers of Christ's sufferings; that, when his glory shall be revealed, ye may be glad also with exceeding joy (1 Pet 4:12–13).

Lord of the Sabbath (2:13–28)

[T]hey that are in old Adam are old creatures; and are in their old things, old ways, old worships, and old religions, and have the old garments, and the old bottles, that hold the old wine, and cannot endure the new; and have the old, rusty, moth-eaten treasure. And they that are in Christ, the heavenly and spiritual second Adam, who maketh all things new, are new creatures, and spiritual men, and are heavenly-minded, and are new bottles, that hold the new wine and the new heavenly treasure, and have the new clothing, the fine linen, the righteousness of Christ, and are the new and living way, over all the dead ways.

—George Fox

Although the warning Jesus gives his disciples to "beware of the leaven of the Pharisees" will not appear in this book for another six chapters (Mark 8:15), it is in this chapter, chapter 2, that we are given several examples of this false form of spiritual edification, along with Jesus's opposition to and correction of the error.[1] In this essay, I will be examining the chapter's conflicts one-by-one to show how Jesus challenges the misuse of the tradition by which the religious authorities hinder the very thing the tradition was

---

1. Epigraph. Fox, *Works*, 8:157. The King James Version is used throughout this essay.

intended to foster, i.e., the spiritual rising to life in Christ. At the end of the essay, I will touch upon the appearance of this same problem in modern-day Quakerism.

HEARING THE CALL (13-14)

The first scene in this chapter positions Jesus at the seaside: a vast, undifferentiated landscape where he teaches a vast, undifferentiated multitude. One verse later, the scene has shifted: Jesus is walking along, and he sees and calls an individual. It is a tax collector, one recognized by all as separate from society. "Follow me," Jesus says to Levi, the son of Alphaeus, and the man, named and individuated, "arose and followed him" (14). The lesson to be taken from the first two verses in this passage is Christ teaches the multitude, but it is the individual whom he calls to follow him, i.e., to find and take up his way of being. Each person—we are being told—must locate and follow the truth within his own heart, regardless of the personal or social ramifications that surely will follow. He or she must honor the integrity of his God-given soul and reject the stance that he is justified by unsubstantiated, traditional ideas or by fitting into his social group. Those who do so will fail to hear the Light, Jesus Christ's transcendent call within to follow him.

NEEDING THE PHYSICIAN (15-17)

In verses 15 through 17, the setting has moved to the house of the called one, where "many publicans and sinners" who "followed" Jesus dine with him and his disciples. Here near the start of his ministry, Jesus's conflict with institutional religion shows itself: the religious authorities imply that eating with publicans and sinners is a violation. Jesus disregards not Mosaic Law but the "tradition of the elders" (7:3): religious precepts long held necessary for righteous life.[2] Jesus responds to the Pharisees' challenge:

---

2. "The Greek word [for tradition] . . . translates 'a giving over,' either by

Lord of the Sabbath (2:13-28)

> They that are whole have no need of the physician, but they that are sick: I came not to call the righteous, but sinners to repentance (17).

In but a few words, Jesus not only sets out his healing mission (introducing the metaphors of health for salvation and sickness for sin) but rebukes those who proudly, erroneously refuse to see their own soul's sickness (their unrighteousness), and thus exempt themselves from recognizing their need of the physician. Only the humble self-aware who feel their alienation from God (i.e., sin) will welcome the physician's care and thus be restored to health and wholeness.

Isaac Penington spoke of "the physician [who] is come inwardly and spiritually"[3] when he wrote the following:

> the broken and humble-hearted ones (who have felt the inward power of life to change their natures, and to preserve them in that which God hath begotten in them), the grace prevaileth to save in every dispensation.[4]

For seventeenth-century Friends, the willingness to recognize the truth of one's inward condition was the crucial requirement through which the soul was prepared for salvation.

Again, Penington describes Jesus Christ and his work:

> [H]e inwardly heals and restoreth his people, faithfully seeking after the sick, the distressed, the broken, the wounded; pouring oil into their wounds, and healing them. But there are some who are so sound and whole

---

word of mouth or in writing; then that which is given over, i.e., tradition, the teaching that is handed down from one to another. The word does not occur in the Hebrew Old Testament (except . . . [when] used in another sense . . .) but is found 13 times in the New Testament . . . . It means, in Jewish theology, the oral teachings of the elders (distinguished ancestors from Moses on) which were reverenced by the late Jews equally with the written teachings of the Old Testament, and were regarded by them as equally authoritative on matters of belief and conduct. . . . [These include] some oral laws of Moses (as they supposed) given by the great lawgiver in addition to the written laws." (Williams, *Encyclopaedia*, 5:3004).

3. Penington, *Works*, 3:278.
4. Penington, *Works*, 2:349.

in their notional apprehensions and practices, that they have no need of the physician, and them the physician passeth by, as unworthy of him, and whom he intendeth shall have no share with him. "Ephraim is joined to idols" (he is well, he hath enough, he hath no need of me) "let him alone," saith the Lord.[5]

THE BRIDEGROOM (18-22)

In this passage, the authorities reproach Jesus for lack of holiness by calling attention to his disciples' failure to fast, as do their own disciples and those of John the Baptist (18). Implied is their assumption that fasting, or asceticism, evinces holiness. Rather than downplaying his disciples' lack of ascetic practice, Jesus capitalizes on it: By referring to himself as "the bridegroom" (19), he alludes to the wedding ceremony where feasting, not fasting, is in order. Jesus's use of the bridegroom metaphor would rile the authorities further in that it would suggest to them that Jesus was making himself equal to God. For in their Scriptures, "bridegroom" was used metaphorically to signal God's relationship to the soul: "[a]s the bridegroom rejoiceth over the bride, so shall thy God rejoice over thee" (Isa 62:5b).

In speaking immediately after of "a piece of new cloth on an old garment" (21), Jesus appears to continue his reference to Isaiah, where in 61:10, the prophet refers both to the marriage ceremony and to "the garments of salvation" (italics mine):

> I will greatly rejoice in the Lord, my soul shall be joyful in my God; for he hath clothed me with *the garments of salvation*, he hath covered me with the robe of righteousness, as a bridegroom decketh himself with ornaments, and as a bride adorneth herself with her jewels.

As do the religious authorities, Jesus knows the Scriptures and the tradition. He uses his knowledge, however, more deftly than they because he understands the true intent and purpose of the

---

5. Penington, *Works*, 3:278.

tradition and thus goes beyond their mere retention of its words and history.

PRIORITIES (23-28)

The final episode in this chapter features many of the same circumstances that have already been reviewed in this essay: the Pharisees challenge Jesus for his disciples' failure to honor the tradition (24), and Jesus retorts by showing not only knowledge of the tradition but his superior, irrefutable understanding of its intent and function (27). The tradition's intent has always been to prepare souls for unity with God, which unity is a person's health and salvation. The tradition was never to be an end in itself: a stand-alone prescription for righteousness that the religious authorities have made of it. The last verse in this chapter presents the maxim that shows the precedence given to the salvation of man—to become "the Son of man"—over traditional practices, such as the sabbath, that were put in place as a means to that end: "the Son of man is Lord also of the sabbath" (28).

For religious communities to make secondary principles and virtues their guidelines for righteousness is a human tendency that extends throughout history, and so Jesus's exposure and correction, as shown in Mark 2, is needed in every age. In our own Quaker communities, such erroneous principles take the form of what twentieth-century Friend Lewis Benson called "cults": "the cult of love and good will," "the cult of the Power of Non-violence," and "the Cult of the Beloved Community" being a few examples that Benson identifies.[6] These take precedence over the call to truth and righteousness that must be promoted, as the Discipline of Ohio Yearly Meeting (Conservative) states.[7]

---

6. Benson writes: "They are all notions and collectively they absorb and deflect the interest, energy, and devotion that should be conserved and redirected if we are to fulfill the purpose for which God called us to be a people." (Wallace, ed. *None*, 56-58).

7. Advise 13 from the *Book of Discipline* of Ohio Yearly Meeting (Conservative) reads: "Make it your aim to promote the cause of truth and righteousness,

Before truth and righteousness can be promoted, however, they must be sought, known, and followed—as Levi followed Jesus in this passage (14). Devotion to secondary principles that supplant the pursuit of truth and righteousness—such as notional ideals of peace, love, and community—is shown to be idolatry when challenged by the writings of Scripture or that of seventeenth-century Friends. Those who idolize the virtue of love ironically exhibit the greatest enmity when challenged and, like the Pharisees, will often conspire against those who honor truth. Laid bare, the foundation of their faith is found to be not the God of Truth but the aspiration to replace him with their own notional ideals.

Yes, peace, love, and community are fine qualities and valued among Christians and Quakers, but they must be authentically received, a consequence of coming into the knowledge of God; they cannot be attained through man's aspiration, which can only be a facsimile that is rooted in pride, to "be as gods, knowing good and evil" (Gen 3:5).

To know and honestly admit to one's state is the essential thing: has one known that Spirit of Christ or has one not known that Spirit? This is an essential act of discernment that requires a truthfulness that too many in Quaker communities would prefer not to venture into, and so they don't. The prophet helps others to see when that essential self-reflection has not yet been undertaken, as Jesus shows the Pharisees and scribes in this passage. In any age, those who undertake the same work can expect the same resistance and personal attacks that Christ's prophets have always endured.

> The Christians formerly (in the first day of the breaking forth of God's power) had Christ in them, the living Word; they opened their hearts to him, received him in, felt him there, found him made of God to them their wisdom, their righteousness, their sanctification, their redemption. They had the thing that those words signify and speak of, and knew the meaning of the words by

---

and to spread the Kingdom of God at home and abroad. Be ready to take your part fearlessly in declaring His message and in witnessing to His power."

feeling of the thing. But Christians now, in the apostasy, have got several apprehensions from the words, without feeling the thing the words speak of; and there lies their religion. And now the heir is come, holding forth the thing they have all been talking of, all sects upon the earth are mad against him, and would fain kill him. They would not have the living substance . . . but they would have their dead apprehensions from the words live, and their dead forms and practices owned; and the heir of life must come in their way . . . or they will not own him.[8]

---

8. Penington, *Works*, 8:157.

Beyond Idealism (3:1–6)

Much that passes as idealism is . . . disguised love of power.
—Bertrand Russell

Last First Day (Sunday), I joined a group of Friends for Bible study an hour before worship at annual sessions of Ohio Yearly Meeting (Conservative). The text before us was Mark 3:1–6 in which Jesus heals a man with a withered hand and evokes the ire of the Pharisees:

> And he entered again into the synagogue; and there was a man there which had a withered hand. And they watched him, whether he would heal him on the sabbath day; that they might accuse him. And he saith unto the man which had the withered hand, Stand forth. And he saith unto them, Is it lawful to do good on the sabbath days, or to do evil? To save life, or to kill? But they held their peace. And when he had looked round about on them with anger, being grieved for the hardness of their hearts, he saith unto the man, Stretch forth thine hand. And he stretched it out: and his hand was restored whole as the other. And the Pharisees went forth, and straightway took counsel with the Herodians against him, how they might destroy him.[1]

---

1. Epigraph. Russell, Nobel Lecture. Mark 3:1–6 (King James Version [KJV]; all subsequent citations are from this version unless otherwise noted.)

Beyond Idealism (3:1-6)

The first two verses of this passage introduce the short narrative's two strands of interest: (1) a man is to be healed, and (2) there's conflict between Jesus and the Pharisees. In verse 3, Jesus prioritizes the first of these two—that is, the healing—by first giving his attention to the man with the withered hand and telling him to "Stand forth." Though given initial priority, the healing is primarily a catalyst to precipitate the main plot line of this story: the conflict between Jesus and the Pharisees.

After having spoken to the man, Jesus turns to the Pharisees and rhetorically asks: "Is it lawful to do good on the sabbath days, or to do evil: To save life, or to kill?" (4) With this question, Jesus identifies opposing principles: do good and save life or do evil and kill. Having defined the two conflicting positions, Jesus then demonstrates through the healing which of the two he upholds; that is to say, he is on the side of doing good and saving life. Seeing the demonstration, the Pharisees are left to conclude on which of the two sides their opposition to Jesus puts them, and they must realize that they occupy the side of doing evil and killing. The verse that follows confirms this fact: "And the Pharisees went forth and straightway took counsel with the Herodians against him, how they might destroy him" (6).

The person of today may read this story and quickly judge the Pharisees to be inexcusably wrong in their insistence on the Law with its hard-and-fast Sabbath rules: that this error was something from long ago and we have progressed well beyond. I propose, however, that the present-day elevation of ideals to the position of primary guiding force of individual or corporate life is but a re-enactment of the Pharisees mistake: both Law and ideals are secondary ethical standards that usurp the central place of Christ, both within a person and within the religious group. Where Christ should be central, ideals are instead rallied around. As was shown in this brief story at the beginning of Mark 3, such usurpation will inevitably entail hostility toward the true standard of righteousness: Christ, the Lord our righteousness (Jer 33:16).

Although the Law of Moses is no longer weaponized to ensure conformity in and manageability of religious communities, different ideals—peace, love, and community—occupy the pedestal in both Liberal and Christian groups. Psychological techniques have replaced physical violence as the means to compel conformity and self-censorship.

In some Christian groups, Jesus is presented as vapidly sweet, and never as he appears in Revelation where he is "called Faithful and True," from whose mouth issues "a sharp sword with which to smite the nations" (19:12,15 [NEB]).[2] All the while in passages such as the one at the beginning of Mark 3, we see Jesus exercising that sword as he puts in place the culprits who hide their love of power behind the guise of ideals. Jesus looks at them with anger and sorrow at their obstinate stupidity (5).

"STRETCH FORTH THINE HAND."

It is the man with the withered hand whom Jesus heals. The hand is the means by which man can make or do; it is the means by which a person can express outwardly what is within: that is, it is the means by which one creates. Symbolically, Christ's restoration of the hand tells of the person's newfound gift to bring forth what is within: that it may become visible to the world.

---

2. This citation is from the New English Bible (NEB).

On Unity (3:20–35)

To all Friends who are in the unity, which is in the light; walk in the light. It is one light that doth convince you all; and one Christ, that doth call all to repentance, up to himself the one head, which is Christ.

—George Fox

The passage in Mark 3:20–35[1] is so complex with its various examples of unity and disunity that it is hard to know where to begin! Implied throughout the text, however, is a single, fixed theme: unity with the Holy Spirit provides strength, while separation from that Spirit ensures weakness and failure.

The topic of unity is set forth at the beginning of the passage in verse 20 where we read: "the multitude cometh together again." Though the multitude is "together" (in unity), they are without Christ and thus seek him. Without Christ, they are weak, even though they are gathered together. We are told "they could not so much as eat bread," which is to say, they cannot sustain themselves.

In the verse that follows, verse 21, Jesus's friends enter the scene. Friends are those with whom we feel some unity. These friends, however, are not in unity with Jesus, and even go so far as to assert that Jesus himself is divided; they say of him, "He is

---

1. Epigraph. Fox, *Works*, 7:58. The King James Version is used throughout this essay.

beside himself" (21). Finally, adding to the muddle, a third group enters: the scribes, who claim Jesus is in unity with "the prince of devils" (22).

As each of the three groups—the multitude, the friends, and the scribes—enters the scene, the situation worsens into confusion, error, and malice. The crowd is unable to order itself to meet its basic needs; Jesus's friends undermine him; and the scribes demonize him. The situation is one of disorder, ignorance, and hostility.

One feels a sense of relief when Jesus begins to speak. We know that he will bring clarity and truth to the chaos spread out before us; his words bring order and peace. For through the Logos, God created the heaven and the earth, and through the Logos the world can be restored to its godly estate in gospel order. Seventeenth-century Friend Robert Barclay in his *Apology for the True Christian Divinity* refers to "common principles of natural truths [that] do move and incline the mind to a natural assent."[2] Even in his unredeemed state, man is capable of reason and assent to natural truths.

And so, Jesus begins with reason. The scribes have charged him with casting out devils by means of unity with the prince of devils (22). Jesus repels the charge with logic (specifically, the first principle of identity, $A = A$): he rhetorically asks the scribes how can he be in unity with Satan when he counteracts Satan by healing the demonically possessed? "How can Satan cast out Satan?" (23) Jesus disarms his opponents by compelling them to see the contradiction or disunity in their thought. He carries the idea further with illustration: "a kingdom . . . divided against itself, that kingdom cannot stand. And a house be divided against itself, that house cannot stand" (24 and 25). In order to be sustained and continue, any being, any entity, any thing—be it a spirit, a thought, a house, or a kingdom—must be in unity with itself: its identity whole and not fragmented by counterforce. Even "if Satan rise up against himself, and be divided, he cannot stand, but hath an end"

---

2. Barclay, *Apology*, 22.

On Unity (3:20-35)

(26). Jesus therewith dismisses the scribes' accusation by means of logic, a method amenable to their predilection.

Continuing with the theme of unity versus division, Jesus deepens the dialogue in the next verses to show the need for unity with the Lord, not opposition to him. In the brief parable that follows, the Lord enters the strong man's house (man harboring of the spirit of Satan), binds the strong man, and spoils his house (Satan's residing within man).

> No man can enter into a strong man's house, and spoil his goods, except he will first bind the strong man, and then he will spoil his house. Verily I say unto you, All sins shall be forgiven unto the sons of men, and blasphemies wherewith soever they shall blaspheme: But he that shall blaspheme against the Holy Ghost hath never forgiveness, but is in danger of eternal damnation (27-29).

It is blasphemy to slander another by calling the true Spirit that empowers him false, but if done in ignorance, the blasphemy is forgivable. *To knowingly slander* the true Spirit in another—to call it false—destroys the slanderer's soul. Denying the Spirit of Truth within oneself likewise puts one "in danger of eternal damnation" (29).

We read in the next verse Jesus's reason for presenting this lesson: "Because they [had] said, He hath an unclean spirit" (30). He has been reproved by his friends ("He is beside himself" [21]) and slandered by his enemies ("by the prince of devils casteth he out devils" [22]). His unity with the Spirit of Truth/Logos has empowered him to refute the scribes' charge and caution his friends about their ignorant error. Finally, in the last few verses of this chapter (31-35), he provides the order necessary for a society (the multitude) to be sustained.

In the early part of this passage, we were told two things about this group "the multitude": that they had come "together" and "they could not so much as eat bread" (20), which is to say that although people were gathered together (unified), the unity among themselves was insufficient to sustain them. This verse is telling us that without Christ, a social group—though unified among its members—cannot truly be alive: cannot participate in the Life. To be sustained, members of a group must be in unity with the Lord, not simply in unity among themselves.

> There came then his brethren and his mother, and standing without, sent unto him, calling him. And the multitude sat about him, and they said unto him, Behold thy mother and thy brethren without seek for thee. And he answered them, saying, Who is my mother, or my brethren. And he looked round about on them which sat about him, and said, Behold my mother and my brethren! For whosoever shall do the will of God, the same is my brother, and my sister, and mother (31–35).

By refusing the call of his family to come away from his work and accompany them, Jesus refutes the authority claims of all social groups. For if the family's demand is set aside (the family being the principal social group), then must *every* social group's demands likewise be considered secondary. Jesus upends the social group's dominant hold upon people (or screen for them) by setting aside the one social group (the family) where natural ties and obligations are the strongest. He reorients kinship (unity) away from natural, social groupings and establishes it anew; kinship is now founded upon knowledge of and obedience to God: "For whosoever shall do the will of God, the same is my brother, and my sister, and mother" (35). Jesus thereby directs people away from the natural tendency to find strength in numbers (social groups) and instead refers them to the power that can order and sustain them each under his own vine and fig tree (Mic 4:4): that is to say, in the power of God.

In an earlier essay, "Beyond Idealism," I wrote of some Christians' preference for presenting Jesus as the facilitator of a smooth, easy flow of omnipresent love from on high to all sinners below. This notion dulls the conscience of the many and extends the influence of the few who perpetrate the claim, for the "people love to have it so" (Jer 5:31). Jesus, however, says nothing of the kind: not in this passage, nor in general, nor is he presented as such by early Friends. Jesus doesn't lull man into somnolence but awakens

On Unity (3:20-35)

him to greater clarity and insight. He calls everyone to a higher way of being that requires the substance of Truth. His example will not let the conscientious person who loves truth continue in the well-worn, unexamined tracks of the millennia, plod out for us wearily to follow. On the contrary, his inward presence enables us to join with him, in spirit and in truth. Therein is the one, true, and miraculous unity.

On Parables (4:1–34)

If you don't eat your meat, you can't have any pudding! How can you have any pudding if you don't eat your meat!

—Pink Floyd

ANYONE WHO HAS LISTENED to *Another Brick in the Wall (part 2)*[1] will not forget the words the distraught teacher screams at the child. The teacher intends to maintain order (as well as control) by enforcing the rule: eat your meat, and you can have your pudding. What makes the scene funny, as well as tragic, is the man's blindness to the absurdity of his full-throated enforcement of this petty rule. His behavior is absurd because he destroys the very thing his role as teacher requires him to preserve: good order in the classroom and healthy, flourishing children. The man has lost sight of the true purpose and meaning of his role and responsibility.

It takes a short leap of imagination to project the dynamic of this classroom fiasco onto the larger screen of society: the school becomes the society, and its rules are replaced by society's laws, manners, and mores. "Eat your meat" becomes: Comply, and do the things that make these laws, manners, and mores second nature to you, and that will allow you to fit in and progress within the society (have your pudding). The problem that ensues, however, is

---

1. Epigraph Pink Floyd, *The Wall*. All biblical citations are from the King James Version.

On Parables (4:1-34)

the growing blindness to life's larger, true purpose, which becomes obscured by the determination to gobble endlessly life's petty puddings. Like the teacher, the child may develop into an adult who unquestionably shuts out the light that lies beyond the bricked-in cave that he and his society have unwittingly, absurdly chosen to inhabit. How do we reach those who see no further than their society's ways (be it those of culture, tribe, or faith community) and have neither ability nor desire to think, feel, or see into the true realm of light and life?

ENTER THE PARABLE

> All these things are done in parables: That seeing they may see, and not perceive; and hearing they may hear, and not understand; lest at any time they should be converted, and their sins should be forgiven them.[2]

No more direct than this explanation is the method by which the parable does its work. Using guerilla tactics, the parable avoids the road of well-traveled and defended ideas, and travels alongside on a path forged by its own narrative. In metaphorical disguise, it draws close to what its hearers have refused to see and have kept hidden. Slipping past the guard of inward blindness, it presents a spiritual truth to be recognized and acknowledged: so that "they should be converted, and their sins should be forgiven them." (This verse [12] cleverly alludes to the resistance of the heart that is "fat," the ears that are "heavy," and the eyes that are "shut" [Isa 6:9–10] to the person's own best interest: i.e., that their sins be forgiven them. Such "heavy" resistance can be overcome through the parabolic ploy.)

Jesus uses the parable to teach of the mystery of the kingdom of God unto them that are without (11). Through metaphor, the parable functions to evoke a recognition of its hearers' inward, spiritual condition. In verses 13–20, Jesus rehearses the particulars of the parable of the sower, which he's given to the multitude, and

---

2. Mark 4:11b–12. (King James Version; all subsequent citations are from this version.)

shows his disciples each particular's corresponding, inward condition. Point by point, he correlates the type of soil onto which the sower's seed is cast to the kind of soul to whom the Word of God is preached.

The long parable of the sower and the equally long explanation of its meaning has been a lesson for his disciples on the objective and strategy of parables. This beginning twenty-verse segment is then followed by a series of short, one- or two-verse parables or metaphors that quickly follow one upon another. It's as if Jesus has patiently explained how parables work and is now presenting example after example of their use in teaching of the kingdom "unto them that are without" (11).

The remaining verses in this passage (21–34) are cast into five segments. Four of the five begin with similar introductory phrases. "And he said unto them" is the phrase that begins both verses 21 and 24; "And he said" is the phrase that starts both verses 26 and 30. Each time one of these introductory phrases appears, the reader is cued a new parable or metaphor is beginning. The first segment (21–23) begins:

> And he said unto them, Is a candle brought to be put under a bushel, or under a bed? And not to be set on a candlestick? For there is nothing hid, which shall not be manifested; neither was anything kept secret, but that it should come abroad. If any man have ears to hear, let him hear.

Both the sower parable that came before and this candle metaphor call a person to take stock of himself: What is the condition of your soul (soil), the sower parable asks. Am I bringing forth light into the world, or am I hiding what I've been given, prompts the metaphor of the candle. In verse 22, however, Jesus opens the possibility that not only goodness and light are within; his reference to hiding, secrecy, and exposure (22) implies that darkness, not light, can prevail within. In this first segment, Jesus has moved from encouraging his hearers to warning them: whether it be good or evil, what resides within will become outwardly manifest.

ON PARABLES (4:1-34)

Capping this three-verse segment is the phrase "If any man have ears to hear, let him hear" (23). The statement introduces a new metaphor: "to hear," meaning "to give one's attention to." He chides his audience to not excuse themselves from attending to his words.

THE SECOND SEGMENT (24-25)

> And he said unto them, Take heed what ye hear: with what measure ye mete, it shall be measured to you: and unto you that hear shall more be given. For he that hath, to him shall be given: and he that hath not, from him shall be taken even that which he hath.

Jesus continues to warn of looming, inevitable justice: what one hears, i.e., what one attends to, will determine not only one's behavior but the content of one's inner being. The true substance of being—the Truth as it is in Christ—is worthy of attention, and attending to that Truth guarantees its beneficial increase. Conversely, attending to that which is without substance—lies from the father of lies—will leave one empty and bereft of existential meaning, even the meaning that one has self-generated. Whatever spirit one harbors will grow or spread within consciousness, eventually to subsume one's entire being: one's will, emotion, mind, and body.

THE THIRD SEGMENT (26-29)

> And he said, So is the kingdom of God, as if a man should cast seed into the ground; And should sleep, and rise night and day, and the seed should spring and grow up, he knoweth not how. For the earth bringeth forth fruit of herself; first the blade, then the ear, after that the full corn in the ear. But when the fruit is brought forth, immediately he putteth in the sickle, because the harvest is come.

With this new parable, Jesus focuses once again on the benevolent "kingdom of God." As in the previous segment, he stresses the incremental growth of life within, and here offers an illustration: through stages, the seed grows into "the full corn." Man "knoweth not how" this growth comes to be: thus Jesus draws attention to the One who is beyond comprehension, who reigns and enables our growth, and we are both the harvest and its beneficiaries: his creation and his image.

THE FOURTH SEGMENT (30-32)

> And he said, whereunto shall we liken the kingdom of God? Or with what comparison shall we compare it? It is like a grain of mustard seed, which, when it is sown in the earth, is less than all the seeds that be in the earth: But when it is sown, it groweth up, and becometh greater than all herbs, and shooteth out great branches; so that the fowls of the air may lodge under the shadow of it.

Building upon the previous segments' teaching of incremental growth, this new parable tempers the idea by warning not to ignore small promptings: it "is less than all the seeds that be in the earth." The spirit of Truth doesn't assist one in acquiring the goods—both material and immaterial—that society worships, and it is therefore usually overlooked or bypassed. Yet if tended to, the seed of Truth grows into a tree "shoot[ing] out great branches" in which the restless flight of being can "lodge."

In the last segment (33-34) of this passage on parables, the narrator himself speaks:

> And with many such parables spake he the word unto them, as they were able to hear it. But without a parable spake he not unto them; and when they were alone, he expounded all things to his disciples.

The narrator has provided readers with a summary of Jesus's teaching method: with the crowd, he uses figurative language: parable and metaphor; with his disciples, he explains the spiritual meaning of his stories and images. A storyteller or artist of any kind must inwardly sense the nature of the substance he would make visible

On Parables (4:1–34)

or sensible to others, and he must faithfully assess whether his expression is true to that inward sense: if he is, in fact, meting that measure (24). Jesus's parables bear an exactitude to the Spirit that testifies to the clarity and strength of the inward vision bestowed upon him. This passage in chapter 4 of Mark is rich and alive with wisdom from above. To enter into its language and thought is to be replenished with the power and beauty of the mind of Christ.

The Other Side (4:33–41)

And with many such parables spake he the word unto them, as they were able to hear it. But without a parable spake he not unto them: and when they were alone, he expounded all things to his disciples. And the same day, when the even was come, he saith unto them, Let us pass over unto the other side (33–35).

THE OPENING VERSES OF this passage point to Jesus's awareness of differing powers of apprehension, and his adapting his teaching method to accommodate each. To the multitude, Jesus has spoken the Word in parables "as they were able to hear it" (33). To the disciples, "he expounded all things" (34), indicating Jesus thought his disciples could better see the correlation between figurative language and spiritual conditions. In the final verse, verse 35, Jesus directs his followers to new territory in which the literal mind of the multitude and the disciples' intellectual grasp of analogy are both transcended. This verse foreshadows a coming into a new kind of understanding that is neither literal nor intellectual but is gained through inward experience and accompanies being itself. Jesus beckons: "Let us pass over unto the other side" (35).

The story begins in a matter-of-fact way: the multitude is "sent away"; there are "other little ships" (36) in the crossing; "a great storm" (37) comes up; and Jesus sleeps comfortably before

The Other Side (4:33-41)

he's awakened by the disciples, who fear for their lives (38). There's nothing in this opening description to alert us that these particulars are anything but facts that describe outward events of time and place. Nothing here seems extraordinary.

It is not until Jesus rises and rebukes the wind and the sea, saying "Peace, be still" (39), that we realize we have moved beyond the mundane and into other territory. The account is no longer a literal description—though the multitude may claim it so; it has shifted into a space where nature neither rules nor sets the bounds of the possible; in this space—on this "other side"—man prevails over nature.

This passage began as a recounting of events taking place in time and space, but having moved past these confines of nature, the passage reveals itself to be a parable, and thus it has an inward, spiritual significance. As a parable, it correlates objective reality with inward states; Jesus Christ performs an outward act (he overcomes the threat of nature—here a storm at sea) that correlates to man's overcoming his inward nature: that of a suffering, storm-tossed creature, fearfully aware of his own mortality. As a parable, man mastering outward nature, as Christ does here, signifies humankind's overcoming and transcending the nature of our being.

Just as the multitude was given parables to bring them to an awareness of their spiritual condition, we are here given to understand that through hearing the commanding Word, Christ within, we may overcome fear and anxiety, our inward "storm," and live in peace.

> And he said unto them, Why are ye so fearful? How is it that ye have no faith? (40)[1]

See how Jesus challenges his disciples to pass into a way of being in which fear has no foothold and faith strides secure. We must leave behind the sure but stodgy ground of the multitude, and embark in darkness upon the watery, formless void, for there is where the Spirit moves and speaks, and it is there that we may receive the light of faith.

---

1. The King James Version is used throughout this essay.

The disciples have yet to learn that they, too, in faith may "pass over unto the other side" (35) and become a different "manner of man" (41). Were it not already verified by personal experience, we could turn to the early Friends to affirm the validity of this teaching.

> To all the elect, chosen and faithful . . . who have not feared the waves of the sea, nor the winds; who fear not the storms nor the weather; whose anchor holds, which is the hope, the mystery, which anchors the soul, which is immortal, to the immortal God.[2]

---

2. Fox, *Works*, 7:157.

The First Workings of the Lord (5:1–20)

But my troubles continued, and I was often under great temptations; and I fasted much, and walked abroad in solitary places many days, and often took my Bible and went and sat in hollow trees and lonesome places till night came on; and frequently in the night walked mournfully about by myself, for I was a man of sorrows in the times of the first workings of the Lord in me. . . . And when all my hopes in them and in all men were gone, so that I had nothing outwardly to help me, nor could tell what to do, then, Oh then, I heard a voice which said, "There is one, even Christ Jesus, that can speak to thy condition."

—GEORGE FOX

IN THE MARK 5 story of the Gadarene demoniac, we are given an intimate look at the soul that has accepted the first workings of the Lord and is thus prepared to hear the voice of Christ. This story is from "the other side," (1)[1] the inward side of life, where one is alone and apart from the give and take, the gratuities and obligations that make up social life. No one wielding social imperatives can bind this solitary man of the tombs, for he has "plucked asunder" all their chains and broken to pieces all their fetters. He will

---

1. Epigraph. Fox, *Journal*, 9–10, 11. The King James Version has been used throughout this essay.

not be tamed (4); nor yield; nor conform to their ways, manners, and customs. Though the man harbors the unclean spirit of the unredeemed and suffers the deathlike despondency of its influence, he tenaciously holds and will not deny the hard truth of his inward condition: he is alienated from God, a truth conveyed in his poignant words: "What have I to do with thee, Jesus, thou Son of the most high God?"(7) It is his willing capacity to see himself as he is that readies him for the "first workings" of the Lord, which mark the man as prepared to receive Christ Jesus.

This honest soul is beleaguered by a contrary force that has claimed preeminence. The man's divided self is evident when he addresses Jesus (italics mine): "I adjure thee *by God*, that thou torment me not" (7). The man calls upon the power of God to limit Christ, the power of God: so muddled is he that the poor man contradicts himself! Firm in his allegiance to truth, yet in the grip of demons, the man is torn and, in his misery, tears himself (5). Legion—his name/self—is victim to forces that appear numerous and controlling; he is fragmented and broken into many parts yet heroically holds himself present to and aware of the misery of his alienated state.

Because the man has not shirked or hidden the truth of his condition from himself, he is able to likewise see the Truth when it appears outwardly, "afar off." Truth as it is in Jesus, he recognizes and runs to worship (6). The man's openness to receiving Truth and Life—when he appears—is proportionate to his having *consciously* endured their prior absence. Though suffering, the man remained faithful to the truth.

In Scripture stories, polarities—such as good and evil, right and wrong, and life and death—are often contrasted, one from the other, through the use of particular motifs. In this story of the demon-possessed man, the motif used to distinguish these opposites is number: Is a word singular or plural? That is to say, "one" signifies what is good: integrated and alive; and "many" signifies what is evil: disintegrated, as in death.[2]

---

2. Note that Jesus's first statement in this story ("Come out of the man, thou unclean spirit" [8]) uses the singular pronoun to address the devil: "thou,"

The First Workings of the Lord (5:1-20)

The protagonist is a solitary man who lives apart from the many in society, and Jesus interacts with him one-to-one. In his first address to the man, Jesus asks his name, using the singular pronoun "thy": "What is thy name?" The man answers: "My name is Legion: for we are many" (9). The man's answer begins with the singular pronoun ("my," not "our") but immediately shifts to a plural pronoun, verb, and adjective: "we are many." This short interchange shows the dispersal into the many of what should be a single, integrated whole: the man's self. The interplay between singular and plural continues through the next sentence (italics mine): "And *he* [the man] besought him [Jesus] much that he would not send *them* [the demons] away out of the country" (10). Again, the singular pronoun (he) is quickly lost to the plural (them) when the demons' will prevails. The poor man cannot speak one coherent sentence without the demons interfering and taking control.

The motif of contrasting the one with the many continues when the devils request entry into the herd of swine. "Herd" signifies the many in which each member has forfeited his own autonomous discernment in order to fit into and be accepted by the many. The herd comprises those who have connected to others as the means to fend off innate, universal loneliness. This existential loneliness, however, can be truly overcome only when the self comes into unity with the spirit of Christ. To elevate group acceptance over one's fidelity to truth is to snap the cord of one's humanity, which is characterized by an alert and open devotion to truth. Those of the herd dismiss the very thing needed for salvation: a soul given to watching for Truth and instead watch for opportunities and threats to their standing and connections within the social sphere. Thus they come to worship the fetters and chains, which, by rights, should be plucked asunder. Unlike the single, distraught man, the herd puts up no resistance to the devils' corruption, and, as a result, they quickly descend to their death

---

not "you." Though the devil will later confuse and debilitate the man by presenting himself as many demons, not one demon, Jesus is able to correctly identify from the start that he is one, signifying the demons' will and character are put in service to one, single end, which is to defy the God of Truth. Though the demons are many and diverse, their purpose is single.

(13),[3] which is to say: spiritual death awaits those who forfeit truth for social connection.

We are told that people from "the city, and in the country" (which is to say, the many)

> went out to see what it was that was done. And they come to Jesus, and see him that was possessed with the devil, and had the legion, sitting, and clothed, and in his right mind [his own integrated self]: and they were afraid. And they [that fed the swine] that saw it told them how it befell to him that was possessed with the devil, and also concerning the swine. And they began to pray him to depart out of their coasts (14–17).

Why should the many be afraid when they see the one has come to himself and is "in his right mind"? The many have chosen a different path: they have foregone the protagonist's solitary trial and have opted instead for the easy, downhill slide of the herd. Seeing the once-possessed man now restored to himself, they are brought face-to-face, each with his own sin: the failure of him- or herself as a human being to be no more than a herd animal, osmotically embodying the communal ethos. Within the group's simulacrum of reality, there is a semblance of a connected life, but it can never reach to the unbounded life and soaring freedom that the blessed, perfected soul enjoys when in unity with the Light of Christ: where we know our true self and the life that the Creator would work within us.

> And they began to pray him to depart out of their coasts (17). . . . [H]e that had been possessed with the devil prayed him that he might be with him (18).

---

3. The herd ran "violently down a steep place" (13) to their death. By having the herd run downhill rather than arduously struggle uphill, the writer conveys the herd's preference for the ease of following the demons' directive, which will be always to descend to a lower or worse condition. By contrast, we read of the protagonist that "always, night and day, he was in the mountains" (5), suggesting a determination in him at all times ("night and day") to ascend to a higher place, in spite of the demons' unrelenting assault.

The First Workings of the Lord (5:1-20)

Here is yet another comparison between the one and the many. The many "pray him [Jesus] to depart out of their coasts," and the one—no longer possessed with the devil—"prayed him [Jesus] that he might be with him." The same dynamic continues through every time and place: those who rely upon the connection with the many would have the Truth depart and trouble them no longer; and those who pray in the privacy of their hearts to be with the Truth are they who, having known the worst the adversary can mount against them, have, nevertheless, endured unto the end (13:13) and known the victory.

Jesus's third and final statement in this story brings together the one and the many but in a new, wholesome configuration. This time the one is not overrun by the hostile, demonic many but instead is to be a single witness, testifying to the many who wish him well. "Go home to thy friends, [says Jesus] and tell them how great things the Lord hath done for thee, and hath had compassion on thee" (19).

> And the light is in the world where all are sinners, but none have the life but who receive it, and are led out of the world by it; to such sheep Christ is keeper, who follow him out of uncleanness . . . but the swine he keeps not, the shepherd they will not follow, there the devil must enter and hath power, and into the sea must they run headlong.[4]

---

4. Nayler, *Works*, 2:210.

A Want of God (5:21–43)

We are a people whom God hath converted to himself... and joined to his own Spirit. We, many of us, sought truly and only after God from our childhood... and knew not how to turn to that of God in us.... By this means we came to great distress and misery beyond all men. Not but that all men were in as great a want of God, his life, power, and presence as we; but the sense thereof was not so quickened in others as in us.

—Isaac Penington

Through the metaphor of suffering and healing, chapter 5 of Mark illustrates the realization of conversion to God. Throughout this chapter in both the first and the second halves, a few individuals stand out as possessing—to use Penington's words—a "quickened" sense of their "want of God"; it is they who are to be healed/converted. Similarly, in both halves of the chapter, the crowd acts as a foil to these individuated persons. It is the herd or throng, those acquiescing to the dominant social consciousness, who openly resist or covertly deny healing through Jesus Christ, the power of God.

In the first half of chapter 5, we visited one whose mind, soul, and heart vividly manifested his "want of God": the Gadarene

A Want of God (5:21-43)

demoniac.[1] By way of contrast, we were also exposed to a group of people who requested Jesus "depart out of their coasts" (17), indicating their refusal to undergo the difficult, solitary trial of entertaining the truth of their inward state, as had the demoniac. In their refusal, they opted for an alternate, less courageous way of being: reliance upon the sanction and acceptance of the tribe or herd. In the story of the Gadarene, the one saved and the many lost function as prototypes: the demoniac demonstrating courageous willingness to undergo transformation/healing, and the herd representing cowardly refusal and enabling conformity.

In the second half of chapter 5 (verses 21 through 43), Jesus has once again "passed over . . . unto the other side," and we are again on that side of the sea where society congregates and crowds form: immediately, we are told that "much people gathered unto him" (21). This is the place where shortly before, Jesus had taught parables to those who see but do not perceive, to those who hear but don't understand (4:12). On this side of the sea, where society comes out in force (24), people lack the inward depth that follows from conscientious self-scrutiny, and instead turn to shallow, social enmeshment.

Jesus's healing work is performed solely within individuals (23-24, 30). Though the crowd on this side of the sea does not bluntly request he leave—as did their Gadarene counterparts (17)—they, nevertheless, deny him. Their collective stance exempts each from acknowledging the deceit that lies within the heart, and consequently there is no sense of personal need for truth: no "want of God." The refusal of the truth in their inward parts disqualifies them all from receiving Jesus's response or healing.

Rather his attention is given to two individuals, the synagogue ruler (22-24) and the woman with "an issue of blood" (25), each of whom expresses his or her own deeply felt need. It is they who stand out from the crowd and receive Jesus's assistance. As

---

1. Epigraph. Penington, *Works*, 1:92-93. See my essay "The First Workings of the Lord (5:1-20)." All subsequent citations in this essay are from the King James Version.

with the demoniac in the first half of the chapter, it is once again individuals who receive Jesus's regard and healing.

Throughout the chapter, those who act collectively are given short shrift. For example, though the crowd presses upon him, he senses and responds only to the touch of the distressed woman who acts in faith (30, 34). To accompany him to the ruler's house (37), he selects only a few disciples, and they are individuated by name: Peter, James, and John. At the house, he sends away the grandstanding weepers and wailers who, lacking sincerity, quickly resort to scornful laughter (38, 40); he again selects only the truly distraught ones, the parents, to enter the healing chamber. Finally, after the healing of the girl, Jesus firmly commands those present not to speak of it to others: "And he charged them straitly that no man should know it" (43). He would stem the contagion of idolatrous faith that quickly spreads through hearsay and, in turn, becomes the dominant social consciousness. Instead, he insists upon authentic faith that arises from the transformative healing itself.

> There are two sorts or degrees of Faith:—the first is, that by which the mind gives its assent to the truth of a thing on the testimony of another; the second is of a more exalted nature, being of Divine origin, and is a gift of the Holy Spirit.[2]

GREATER AND LESSER

In the first half of chapter 5, we saw the most extreme, vivid example of an individual's restoration to Life. In the second half of the chapter, the stark, unembellished battle for the soul is no longer on view, rather we see examples of the suffering that beleaguers every person in the world: the threat of losing what is most dear. In this second half, a prominent man fears the death of his daughter, and a woman fears for her health. Though each is threatened with exceedingly great loss, neither the man nor the woman undergoes the direct attack on the soul that we witnessed earlier in

---

2. Molinos et al. *True Peace*, 17.

A WANT OF GOD (5:21-43)

the Gadarene. The loss of a child or of one's health are two of the most severe losses one can undergo in the world, yet they do not automatically lead to loss of the soul: a lesson also presented in the book of Job.

The division of the chapter midway between the two locations suggests the two passages are in balance: the telling of the demoniac's story is given space equal to the two healing stories in the chapter's second half. Balance or equation between the two halves of the chapter implies the first threat was as severe as the latter two combined. The worst loss in the world—even of child or health—is not as injurious to one's being as is the loss of one's soul, that is to say, the loss of one's connection to God: a lesson also presented in the story of Abraham and Isaac.

In the Gadarene story, the archetypal threat to being (a soul overrun by demons) was illustrated. In the stories of Jairus, the synagogue ruler (22), and the woman with "an issue of blood" (25), we are shown lesser threats. Yet suffering the loss of what is greatly valued can and often does lead to despair, bitter resentment, cynicism, or narcissism: all signaling unbelief and alienation from God.[3] Thus the synagogue ruler hearing his daughter has died (35) is bolstered immediately by the Living One's guidance: "Be not afraid, only believe" (36). Believing that God can and will see us through our deepest losses maintains an open conduit to that infinite Source of strength and well-being: Christ, the power of God.

ESSENTIALS AND INCIDENTALS

In the second half of chapter 5, we have witnessed two individuals' need for God. The writer gives us numerous details about each of them, which we can analyze to find what qualities they have in common and what qualities are particular to each. The common qualities inform us of what is needed for readiness to receive

---

3. [Satan challenges God:] "Thou hast blessed the work of his [Job's] hands, and his substance is increased in the land. But put forth thine hand now, and touch all that he hath, and he will curse thee to thy face" (Job 1:10-11).

Christ's healing in our lives, while the differences signal that each healing occurs within a unique individual in all his particularity. Given our natural propensity to confuse the incidental with the essential,[4] the writer distinguishes between the two by making the essential qualities appear in both characters and the incidental only in one.

Both the ruler and the woman are in need and are confident Jesus can help (23, 28);[5] both believe that touch (connection to or unity with Jesus) will provide the healing they seek (23, 28); both honor Jesus by falling down before him: i.e., subjecting themselves (22, 33); and the healing each of them receives is linked to the number twelve (25, 42), indicating wholeness or completion.[6]

The individuality of the synagogue's ruler and the woman with "an issue of blood" is indicated by their dissimilarities: the ruler is a man of high status, and we're given his name (22), while the woman is among the crowd and anonymous (31); the ruler asks directly for Jesus's help (23), while the woman secretly touches Jesus's clothes (27); Jesus intentionally heals the ruler's daughter (41), while his healing of the woman is accomplished without his knowledge or intent (30). The dissimilarities inform us of qualities

---

4. A blatant example of confusing the incidental with the essential is recorded in Fox's *Journal* where people claim the incidental of gender is an essential determinate in whether or not one possesses a soul: "After this, I met with a sort of people that held women have no souls, adding in a light manner, no more than a goose. But I reproved them and told them that was not right, for Mary said, "My soul doth magnify the Lord, and my spirit hath rejoiced in God my Saviour'" (Fox, *Journal*, 8–9).

5. To apply these essentials to ourselves, it would be appropriate to substitute the word "truth" in place of the word "Jesus," as we have no knowledge of who Jesus is until he appears within, whereas prior to his appearing, we can attempt to discern truth from falsehood. Initially—in the first birth—it is solely to truth that we owe our allegiance. It is the allegiance itself that deepens and readies the soul to receive Jesus Christ.

6. "The number [12] pointed in the first instance to unity and completeness, which had been sanctioned by Divine election, and it retained this significance when applied to spiritual Israel" (Smith, *Encyclopaedia*, 4:2162).

that are incidental to spiritual healing, namely social status, gender, age, and Jesus's consent (30).[7]

CONCLUSION

Chapter 5 of Mark is a lesson in the personal dynamics of salvation. Suffering comes to everyone in this world; it is a given. Our response to that fact of life determines whether or not we are prepared to receive God's merciful resolution. The individual who inwardly reflects upon the truth of his condition and conscientiously endures that truth will become open to receiving God's grace. The many who turn away from the truth to outward, social distraction will come to find that their lives have been no more than a confounded, man-made flight, downed in darkness: without wisdom, without virtue, and without fulfillment. The stakes are high in this life, and we are responsible for meeting the high expectation inherent to our humanity. In Scripture, we have been given guidelines and information on the way forward, particularly in this chapter where options are so clearly delineated. Our progenitors in faith, the early Friends, lived fully into the responsibility that confronts us all.

> Pull down that dead, dark, corrupt image, and mere shadow and shell of Christianity, wherewith Antichrist hath deceived the nations, for which end he hath called us to be a first-fruits of those that serve him, and worship

---

7. Jesus's sensing that "virtue had gone out of him" and not knowing who had "touched [his] clothes" (30) suggests both his "being in the form of God ... and [his being] made in the likeness of men" (Phil 2:6-7). That is to say, he has the virtue (power) of God yet is not all-knowing (Mark 13:32). It is his Spirit that is the operative force in the healing, not his flesh, which "profiteth nothing"(John 6:63). The healing is attributed to the woman's faith, "*Thy faith* hath made thee whole" (34). (Italics are mine.) In this way, the distinction is subtly made that Jesus is to be worshiped as the conveyer (mediator) of the power of God, and not in a fleshly way: as an idol who magically heals physical ailments. Faith is the life and power of God received.

him no more in the oldness of the letter, but in the newness of the spirit.[8]

Oh, the mystery of life! Oh, the hidden path thereof, which none can learn but those whom the Father teacheth! But many think to learn in that, which ever was, and ever will be, shut out. If Christ would lay his doctrine before them, and make it good to their understanding, they would receive it. No, no; they must bow to Christ, to his name, to his power, to his will, to his way of manifesting his truth; he will not bow to theirs.[9]

---

8. Barclay, *Apology*, 480.
9. Penington, *Works*, 4:23.

Gospel Work (Mark 6)

Come ye yourselves apart into a desert place, and rest a while (31).

CHAPTER 6 IN THE book of Mark is a primer on gospel work, which is largely characterized as overcoming the force that possesses fallen humankind. With its 56 verses, the chapter is one of the longest in the book. (The only one longer is chapter 14, which covers the time preceding Jesus's execution.) I've divided this chapter into five segments and titled them as follows: (1) how the work begins, (2) how it progresses, (3) opposition and advancement, (4) overcoming nature, and (5) restoration to wholeness. Though the chapter is comprised of many different scenes and stories, it exhibits one overriding theme: there are ways to handle worldly opposition so that the gospel continues to prosper and, in the end, prevail.

HOW THE WORK BEGINS (1-6)

Chapter 6 begins by placing the story in Jesus's "own country" (1).[1] More specifically, the scene occurs in a synagogue on the sabbath (2): the spiritual center of the culture. Jesus's beginning his ministry at this time and place tells us that gospel work begins when one person—with all his historical-cultural, geographical, and

1. All citations are from the King James Version.

personal specificity—embodies and expresses the Spirit of God. Like the origin on the number line, the starting point for gospel work is the individual—located in time and space—who receives and knows the power of God and is given to speak his wisdom (2): in short, gospel work begins with a prophet.

These first few verses introduce both the beginnings of and the resistance to gospel work, the forces—pro and con—that will appear repeatedly throughout the chapter. In these opening lines, the ministering prophet is met at once with opposition from the congregation, which having heard and recognized his heavenly wisdom (2) nevertheless strives to bind him to earth with ties of trade and kin: "Is not this the carpenter, the son of Mary, the brother of James, and Joses," etc. The group is offended (3) by the prophet's wisdom, perhaps conscious that God has raised up one from among their number, and it hasn't been them! Envy of the prophet is the first opposition expressed in this chapter, as it is likewise presented early in Scripture. The spirit of Cain is characterized by outward religious observance and profession and an accompanying persecution of those who manifest inward, authentic faith. The first lesson in gospel work is to recognize that neither earthly ties nor ill-treatment can stop the work's progress. Opposition will arise from those who profess but do not possess the faith, but the work must continue, even though its pace be slackened:

> And he could there do no mighty work, save that he laid his hands upon a few sick folk, and healed them. And he marvelled because of their unbelief. And he went round about the villages, teaching (5-6).

HOW THE WORK PROGRESSES (7-13)

In verses 7-13, the gospel reach is extended through empowering and delegating the work to others. In this passage, Jesus instructs and enables the twelve disciples to go two by two, to have power over unclean spirits, and to bring certain provisions but not others (7-9). In the next two verses (10 and 11), Jesus continues

Gospel Work (Mark 6)

his instruction, but now it is he himself—not the narrator—who speaks, indicating these spoken commands have more significance than the previously narrated ones. Jesus says:

> In what place soever ye enter into an house, there abide till ye depart from the place. And whosoever shall not receive you, nor hear you, when ye depart thence, shake off the dust under your feet for a testimony against them. Verily I say unto you, It shall be more tolerable for Sodom and Gomorrha in the day of judgment, than for that city (10–11).

The earlier instruction addressed logistics: how the disciples were to travel, supply and clothe themselves, and do their work. The instruction Jesus himself gives in verses 10 and 11 guides the disciples in handling the less tangible problems they will encounter. To abide solely in one house while visiting a community (10) heads off wayward tendencies among the townsfolk, such as competition between hosts, speculation on reasons for the travelers' shifting between households, or discrediting the motives for their travel and visit. For the disciple pairs to remain in one household in each place visited helps both the surrounding community and the disciples themselves to remain focused on what they are there to say and do, rather than become hindered by distractions.

The second piece of advice Jesus gives (to "shake off the dust under [their] feet" [11]) serves to protect the disciples' inward state when they come across rejection. In this instance, Jesus's language is fierce as he teaches the disciples how to respond to those who are unworthy of the gospel message; the disciples' dismissive dust-shaking will testify in heaven, and divine retribution will come upon all who reject the gospel message (11).

This second passage (verses 7–13) follows a back-and-forth pattern: positioning a prediction of resistance between two segments in which the work is advanced: the first, preparing the disciples for the mission (7–10) and the second, telling of their success (12, 13).

ADVANCEMENT AND OPPOSITION (14-44)

Mark 6 is about advancement of and opposition to the work of the gospel, the activity of bringing the power of God to earth, as it is in heaven. The first thirteen verses of the chapter have briefly eyed this progress and resistance. Beginning with verse 14 and continuing through verse 44, however, is the chapter's central exposition, which features an illustration of each of these two opposing forces, each presented in its most pronounced, essential form. The evil opposition mounted against the gospel is represented in verses 14-29: the story of a prophet's execution. By contrast, the second story illustrates the gospel providing sustenance to a multitude: the feeding of the 5,000. The two stories are equal in length, each comprising fifteen verses.

The story of John the Baptist's execution begins in an odd, nonchronological way: we come upon king Herod guiltily obsessing over his part in the prophet's death. Apparently deranged, he repeatedly claims that Jesus is, in fact, John "risen from the dead" (14, 16). Before we readers are launched into the telling of the horrendous events of this crime, we see its perpetrator distraught with guilt. Killing the prophet is the ultimate act of opposition to gospel work, yet at the outset of the tale of the prophet's death, we see one of its perpetrators not elatedly triumphant but debilitated and overthrown by his own sin and crime.

Herod is a man of divided mind: he is in awe of John's righteousness, his holiness; gladly hears John speak (20); and was sorry to execute him (26). These worthy sentiments are countered, nevertheless, by Herod's unbridled pride and lust (22, 26). His inner division weakens him, and he is easy prey for his manipulative and vengeful wife (19), who holds a grudge against the prophet (19) and plots his death (24). Unlike Herod, his wife Herodias entertains neither inward reflection nor guilt prior to or following the death. The dancing daughter, the third accomplice, likewise shows no evidence of inward life; she plays her part and is done. Each of the three has had a role to play in the prophet's demise, and the lesson gospel workers are to learn from this passage is that conspiracy

Gospel Work (Mark 6)

features in the most severe type of gospel resistance (a fact that will be verified later on a grander scale when religious leaders collude with their people and with empire to kill Jesus). The charger, or large platter, that carries the head of the prophet is an emblem of the moral crime of the three, and in verses 27 and 28, the charger is passed among them, touching all three:

> And immediately the king sent an executioner, and commanded his head to be brought: and he went and beheaded him in the prison. And brought his head in a charger, and gave it to the damsel: and the damsel gave it to her mother (27–28).

The charger is significant in another way, for it is a platter for carrying food, and, in fact, John's beheading has occurred during a feast. We are being told that the death of the prophet is food for the demonic, gospel-resenting spirit. It is no accident that the story that follows—the feeding of the 5,000—also centers on food. In each story, the type of "food" is appropriate to the nature of the spirit it sustains. In the first story, death feeds the demonic spirit. In the second, "food" is blessed by one who looks up to heaven and leaves all who eat filled with sustenance (41–42): filled and sustained by the Living Word.

Before getting into the main portion of the second story—feeding the multitude—we're first given a brief introductory passage, which parallels the earlier introduction to the story of the prophet's death that featured the king's anxious, demoralized state. The brief introduction to the second story shows the disciples returning from their mission, gathering to Jesus, and telling him "what they had done, and what they had taught" (30). Unlike the earlier dark introduction with its deranged king guiltily ruminating over what he had done, the introduction to the second story shows the disciples' eager and joyful recounting of what *they* had done in their travel. Jesus then encourages them to rest in solitude, before they get on with the work of responding to "many coming and going" (31), who want to hear the gospel message. The second introduction brims with jubilant, purposeful, caring, light-filled comradery, which is in high contrast to the king's guilty, solitary rumination.

The contrast between these two stories is striking, and the narrator accentuates that contrast by using the same format (introduction before the story proper), as well as the same motif (feeding), in both. This technique serves to underscore the many differences between the two stories: in setting; tone; plot; and, most of all, in the spirit of the characters who inhabit each. The settings are different: "a desert place" contrasted with the king's palace. The class of people who spontaneously and eagerly seek and run afoot to gather to hear Jesus contrasts with the elite society invited (summoned?) to the king's celebration of himself on his birthday. The worldly king is subject to his wife's manipulation, the girl's wishes, and his guests' favorable opinion, while Jesus, the heavenly king, is subject to no one. After hearing the disciples' command, "Send them away" (36), Jesus ignores it and counters with a command of his own, "Give ye them to eat" (37). Herod is unable to lead even his own household, while Jesus compassionately takes on the role of shepherd to an assembled crowd of strangers. While the prophet's head is brought from a dark prison to a dark banquet hall; the feeding of the five thousand occurs in the open air with heaven above and the food blessed. The death of the prophet John is a great loss that figuratively feeds but a few condemned souls; while the prophet's speaking the living Word—though he has but little (five loaves and two fishes)—is able to feed and fill a great many. To drive home the point of abundance, we're told the disciples "took up twelve baskets full of the fragments, and of the fishes" (41–44).

OVERCOMING NATURE (45–52) AND RESTORATION TO WHOLENESS (53–56)

Chapter 6 has a symmetrical structure: two short segments, each approximately half a dozen verses, begin the chapter; they are followed by one lengthy central portion, illustrating first resistance to and then advancement of the gospel work; and finally, two additional short passages complete the chapter, balancing the narrative structure by mirroring the two short segments at the beginning. On either side of the central main portion of the chapter are two short passages.

In the first of these two ending passages (45–52), Jesus is shown to be in command: putting disciples into a ship and sending away the people (45). Though he directs and sustains others, he himself must turn to God for direction and restoration, and so "he departed into a mountain to pray" (46). Readers are then immediately taken to a night scene where disciples row upon the sea and are troubled by heavy wind. In this vignette, we see the same necessity for reliance upon the Lord (48) that Jesus exhibited in the scene immediately before: in his going to a mountain to pray.

The disciples' struggle with nature speaks of the need for assistance: they are out of control and afraid. Their situation symbolically represents human nature in its fearful reaction to being overpowered and out of control. Jesus overcomes human nature, symbolically represented by his overcoming our natural incapacity to walk upon water (49). He hears the disciples cry (49), identifies himself (50), and comes into their ship (51). We can take from this miraculous account the correlating lesson that human nature is stilled and at peace (healed) when Jesus appears and comes into the vessel of our soul.[2] As Jesus in prayer relies upon God, so the disciples can rely upon Jesus who restores their "good cheer" (50).

The final verses of this chapter (53–56) rebut the limitation placed upon the work in verse 5, where we were told that Jesus, in "his own country," was unrecognized by the townsfolk and could "do no mighty work save that he laid his hands upon a few sick folk, and heal[ed] them." In these final verses of chapter 6, Jesus

---

2. And he went up unto them into the ship; and the wind ceased; and they were sore amazed in themselves beyond measure, and wondered. *For they considered not the miracle of the loaves: for their heart was hardened* (51–52). (Italics are mine.) Had the disciples had the tendered heart to understand "the miracle of the loaves," they also would have understood the wind's cessation upon Jesus's entering their ship. Each rendition of a miracle correlates outward events with inward, spiritual reality. A heart made tender by Jesus's having entered the soul understands that correlation; whereas hardened hearts do not (52). Once again, we are reminded of early Friends' insistence on the need to read the Scriptures in the same spirit in which they were written.

is recognized for whom he is (54), and, as a result, many sick are brought to him (55). Unlike in the corollary verse early in the chapter in which Jesus could heal only a few (5), at the end of the chapter, he heals those from "villages, or cities, or country" (56); we are being told that Jesus is the universal healer.

As Jesus, the prophet "without honor" (4), began his ministry (as told in this chapter), his work was stymied by people's unbelief and ill-treatment. In chapter 6, we learn that these forces of resistance do not have the last word. Whether the prophetic spirit is raised up in John; in Jesus; in you or me; or in those who come after, we are empowered to persevere in time, undergo persecution, remain diligent, and rely upon the Lord. In doing so, the gospel work goes forward, and the human soul—fractured and fallen—is miraculously healed and made whole, having touched Christ Within.

The Prophet Schooled (Mark 7)

OCCASIONALLY IN SCRIPTURE, WE catch a glimpse of Jesus learning to better perform his work; chapter 7 of Mark gives us one such example. Midway through this chapter is an encounter with a woman from Phoenicia, an area north of Jesus's own region of Galilee. Ironically, this woman teaches Jesus that he's come perilously close to making the same errors with which he had earlier accused the Pharisees and chastened his disciples. Jesus, however, learns from the incident and is then able to carry on his work more effectively.

Chapter 7 has four parts: (1) Jesus lambastes the religious authorities [1–13]; (2) teaches the people and his disciples [14–23]; (3) encounters the Syrophenician woman [24–30]; and, finally, (4) heals the deaf, dumb man [31–37].

JESUS LAMBASTES THE RELIGIOUS AUTHORITIES (1–13)

> Isaiah was right when he prophesied about you hypocrites in these words: "This people pays me lip-sevice, but their heart is far from me: their worship of me is in vain, for they teach as doctrines the commandments of men."[1]

---

1. The version of the Bible I've used here in Mark 7:6 is The New English Bible (NEB). I've also used the King James Version (KJV) in this essay and have indicated in the text which version is cited.

Quoting the prophet Isaiah (29:13), Jesus charges the religious authorities with the all-too-common error of relinquishing the imperative to honor God to practice man-made religion. What interests me in this first passage of the chapter, however, is not Jesus's valid criticism of the authorities. Rather my attention is drawn to what appears to be ebbing power in Jesus's speech, from the beginning of the passage to its end.

After a strong start—quoting the great prophet and succinctly identifying the offenders' spiritual error—Jesus launches into a specific example: i.e., the Corban oath, a man-made addition to the tradition. His lengthy, detailed account of this practice (10–13) seems to convey a pent-up resentment of the authorities' hypocrisy, as it does not address the topic at hand: that his disciples don't wash their hands before they eat (5). Jesus's resentment—though understandable—is a self-indulgent, emotional release. Its spiritual consequence can be monitored through the loss of power in his speech as it progresses. He ends this exchange with the authorities with what appears to be a vague attempt to load on more fault: "And many other things that you do are just like that" (13). It is as if he is trying to regain the force he felt and manifested at the beginning of the exchange.

JESUS TEACHES THE PEOPLE AND HIS DISCIPLES (14-23)

Although Jesus is superb in his use of metaphor to explain that defilement comes from within and not from without, his lack of patience with his hearers—both people and disciples—shows. He asks his disciples, "Are you as dull as the rest?" (18) Regardless of how astonished Jesus is at his hearers' lack of understanding, he does not foster their learning by remarking on the magnitude of their insensibility.

In both beginning episodes of this chapter, Jesus has exhibited great understanding of the faith, but he's shown himself unable to present the wisdom in a way that benefits others; in fact, his presentation thwarts his intent to communicate. With the religious

THE PROPHET SCHOOLED (MARK 7)

authorities, he veers off into a complex description of a different offense, and with the people and disciples, he speaks beyond their ken. He's resentful toward the former, and surprised and annoyed with the latter.

JESUS ENCOUNTERS THE SYROPHOENICIAN WOMAN (24-30)

This pivotal mid-chapter episode begins with Jesus attempting to hide himself from others in a house in Phoenicia (24); one surmises that he was disgruntled with his recent encounters and felt entitled to some respite. We are told that his intention was not met, for "he could not be hid" (24 [KJV]). Here we are subtly reminded that the prophet's will is not always in accord with the Father's, and it is the Father who prevails: a lesson also taught in the tale of Jonah.

In this passage with the Syrophoenician, Jesus's attention is turned once again to the earlier concern of defilement or the "unclean spirit." (It's as if he's given another chance to—this time—get it right.) In comes a woman in great need; her young daughter has an "unclean spirit" (25), and she seeks Jesus's help to "cast forth the devil out of her daughter" (26). Her plea for his help is rebuffed with his harsh words:

> Let the children first be filled: for it is not meet to take the children's bread, and to cast it unto the dogs (27).

Jesus calls the woman, who is seeking his help, a dog; she is a Gentile, a Phoenician of Syria: not of his faith and not of his nation. Just as earlier in the chapter, the religious authorities were bound by man-made, cultural rules, Jesus here is likewise bound by cultural suppositions: namely, it is the children of Israel who alone have the right to the spiritual sustenance God has sent to his people; others, not of this nation, are not worthy of this gift. Similarly, just as the people and disciples were ignorant of the dynamics of defilement, Jesus here shows himself to be ignorant of God's loving Providence for all people.

At this turning point in the chapter's narrative, Jesus is schooled by a Gentile woman of a foreign nation. (Could there be a more humbling circumstance!) To his ignorance and pride, the woman responds with humility: "Yes, Lord: yet the dogs under the table eat of the children's crumbs" (28). The teachable prophet, now humbled, acknowledges her humility and its remediating effect: "For saying that, you may go home content; the unclean spirit has gone out of your daughter" (29 [NEB]).

True humility is a spiritual condition that is located beyond its semblance: the man-made, voluntary counterpart (Col 2:18 [KJV]); humility for humility's sake misses the mark. Neither is one sent to claim ownership of and gratify oneself with the heavenly gifts that have been bestowed. True humility is to suspend the self with its fleshly pride and resentment, for the work to be done must and will originate from the higher and truer Spirit.

JESUS HEALS THE DEAF, DUMB MAN (31-37)

In the first verse of this final passage, we are told that Jesus has left the foreign land and is located in his home country of Galilee (31). He is at home geographically and metaphorically: spiritually at home in his newly recovered humility. He no longer is engaging in diatribes against the hypocrites or marveling at the dullness of the people. In fact, he hardly speaks at all but silently acts to heal humanity one person at a time (33). No longer reacting to the "godforsaken, obscene, quicksand of life,"[2] he instead looks to and settles his mind in heaven, though human sighs and groans still accompany his work (34).

The Aramaic word *"Ephphatha"* is his sole verbalization in this final passage. He now speaks in language that can be understood by those around him: in words that are not beyond the ken of the metaphorically deaf and dumb. His language, the Word, mediates the spiritual separation between heaven and ailing

---

2. Weems, "Jesus Wept."

The Prophet Schooled (Mark 7)

humanity (34–35): "Be opened" is his Word within, his command and pronouncement.

Ending the chapter is the familiar charge that no one be told of the healing. Jesus would have all be open and unprejudiced by stories of his power that inevitably lead to mistaken interpretations and expectations, which cannot be anything but a hindrance to his work. Nevertheless, his command goes unheeded, and the people remain astonished and uncomprehending that he "makes the deaf hear and the dumb speak" (37).

If any man have ears to hear, let him hear (16).

Our Example (Mark 8)

Many other grounds there be that brings not fruit to perfection, who are not found faithful to him that hath called them therein; so that now truth is, that many are called, but few chosen and faithful; many are ashamed at the Lamb's appearance, it is so low & weak & poor & contemptible, & many are afraid seeing so great a power against him; many be at work in their imaginations, to compass a kingdom to get power over sin, & peace of conscience, but few will deny all to be led by the Lamb in a way they know not, to bear his testimony & mark against the world and suffer for it with him.

—James Nayler

Early in Mark's Gospel, we are told that Jesus saw his mission to be traveling to different towns to preach.[1] Although he had healed individuals one by one in his travels, his teaching ministry had grown to the extent that he was reaching thousands at a time: five thousand in chapter 6 and another four thousand in chapter 8. Yet despite the large number fed by his teaching, we do not see him rejoicing in this ministry. On the contrary, throughout the first and major portion of chapter 8, there are hints of Jesus's dissatisfaction, impatience, and growing realization that more is required of him

    1. Epigraph. Nayler, *Works*, 4:9. "And he said unto them, Let us go into the next towns, that I may preach there also: for therefore came I forth" (Mark 1:38). The King James Version is used throughout this essay.

OUR EXAMPLE (MARK 8)

in his sojourn upon the earth. By comparing the events that occur early in this chapter to similar events that have taken place in the preceding two, we see Jesus being led to this difficult realization.

The first nine verses of chapter 8 revisit the feeding of the multitude that occurred in chapter 6; in the next verses, 11–13, the run-in with the Pharisees and scribes from chapter 7 is repeated. His disciples' incomprehension is admonished in verses 16–21, and the healing of the blind man is in verses 22–26, each echoing an event in chapter 7. Although chapter 8 repeats stories from chapters 6 and 7, the events differ in the later rendition, revealing Jesus's changing awareness, moving from prophet to Messiah: from seeing himself as a man to seeing himself as the Son of man.

First, however, let's delve into the details and compare these correlated stories.

THE FEEDING OF THE MULTITUDE (6:33–44 AND 8:1–9)

Both stories in chapters 6 and 8 are set in the wilderness where many people have nothing to eat; Jesus commands them to sit down, and then gives thanks for and blesses the food; his disciples distribute the food, and the people are filled; the remainder is gathered and fills a number of baskets; the people are sent away, and the episode is followed by travel on a ship. These many similarities tell us what is typical, and thus the differences between the stories inform us of the new direction the narrative is taking.

In both stories, it is Jesus's compassion that moves him to meet the people's needs.[2] In the earlier story in chapter 6, however, his compassion arises from seeing the people as sheep not having a shepherd, and he thus begins to teach them. Comparing this with the feeding the multitude story in chapter 8, we see that his compassion arises directly from the people's "hav[ing] nothing to eat."

---

2. Jesus immediately speaks in this chapter of his having "compassion on the multitude" (8:2). In the earlier story, the same reason for assisting the people is given: "when he came out, saw much people, and was moved with compassion toward them" (6:34).

The earlier use of the shepherd metaphor calls for some roundabout mental maneuvering to equate material food with spiritual food (the material food of loaves and fishes is used as metaphor for the spiritual food of Jesus's teaching).[3] In the later story, no such metaphor appears; Jesus states outright: the people "have nothing to eat" (2). This bluntness suggests an impatience on Jesus's part: he is now seeing human need for sustenance is to be met directly, and not circuitously through metaphor. Additionally, he states the people have been with him three days with nothing to eat, indicating he's aware of time's passing and his need to act directly and without delay.

Following the feeding of the multitude in chapter 6, the disciples were put onto a ship, and Jesus went to a mountain to pray before later joining them. In chapter 8, they all debark together (10). The event is condensed, abbreviated, as if there's no time for anything but action. Things need to move forward, get done.

> When I brake the five loaves among five thousand, how many baskets full of fragments took ye up? They say unto him, Twelve. And when the seven among four thousand, how many baskets full of fragments took ye up? And they said, Seven (8:19-20).

The reader is invited to compare the numbers. Previously a larger number were fed with fewer loaves and fishes, and more baskets were retrieved. The later event fed fewer though the supply was greater, and fewer baskets were retrieved. The numbers show a decline in efficacy. The number seven appears twice in the chapter 8 story: both as the number of loaves offered and as the number of baskets of fragments taken up. The number seven signifies completion[4] and is here used to signify that the time is fulfilled;

---

3. A shepherd who feeds sheep is a metaphor for Jesus's teaching spiritual truth to people, a metaphor also used by George Fox: "All . . . who are made alive by Christ Jesus . . . and so are come to feed upon the heavenly and spiritual things, which Christ your shepherd directs you to, according to your capacity, age, and growth: and so to know him that God has sent to feed you, above all the feeders that men have sent" (Fox, *Works*, 8:76).

4. "[T]he number 7, which is referred to in one way or another in nearly

OUR EXAMPLE (MARK 8)

Jesus can no longer continue in the same manner; the time for this kind of work is now finished.

THE RUN-IN WITH THE PHARISEES AND SCRIBES (7:1-13 AND 8:11-13)

When the Pharisees and scribes challenge Jesus in the earlier story, he responds by expanding the discussion into a new topic (the Corban oath), and then he goes into detail about what that is, why it's morally wrong, and that it is not in accord with the intent and spirit of the tradition. When the Pharisees again challenge him in the chapter 8 story, Jesus curtails rather than expands the discussion. He dismisses the Pharisees with one blunt statement, telling them they will not get what they want (12). Jesus seems to have realized that there is nothing to be accomplished by his explaining or interacting with these adversaries.

THE UNCOMPREHENDING DISCIPLES (7:18 AND 8:16-21)

In each of these stories, the disciples fail to understand Jesus's use of metaphor. Spiritual lessons often use metaphor, which relies upon a person's ability to correlate familiar material objects and sensory processes with inward truth or reality; metaphor provides an outline of a real but unseen form.

The reality itself sits like a photograph beneath a sheet of tracing paper, onto which an artist copies barely visible forms. The traced image is an abstraction that suggests the reality hidden beneath. Though without some prior familiarity with the hidden thing itself, the viewer may not be able to make sense of the lines he sees; he may not understand what the drawing represents.

In both of these stories, Jesus expresses surprise that his metaphors do not communicate the hidden, inward reality. In the

---

600 passages in the Bible. . . . [is] the number of totality, of completeness" (Smith, *Encyclopaedia*, 4:2159).

first story in chapter 7, however, he explains and elaborates upon the nature of that reality (18–23), while in the second story, he simply ends the conversation with the words "How is it that ye do not understand?" (21) and makes no further attempt to explain.

THE HEALINGS (7:32–35 AND 8:22–26)

In both of these stories, Jesus removes the one to be healed from the multitude or town (7:33 and 8:23), for he heals individuals, one by one—not groups. In the earlier story, one word, "*Ephphatha*," was sufficient to heal the man. In the correlating story in chapter 8, the healing of the blind man requires two passes: the first attempt doesn't fully work (24). Jesus is finding that his methods of working are not as effective as they were previously, and this signals a need for change. He ends the healing in his typical way: with a charge to tell no one. And here, the slow progress of his work must have been keenly felt.

In these early stories of chapter 8, Jesus has interacted with the people and with adversaries, disciples, and one ready to be healed, and he has repeatedly found a diminished effect. A tone of restless disquietude pervades these stories. The narrator conveys Jesus's growing sense that there's no longer time for elaboration and circuitous methods: things have to change, move forward, get done. That Jesus's method of working no longer seems valid to him is a necessary development for his coming to accept the role of Messiah. The teaching he has done thus far is the work of a prophet, but the Son of man is called to more than prophecy.[5]

He and his disciples walk northward to the towns of Caesarea Philippi (27). The two previous chapters were set either in the tetrarchy of Herod Antipas or in territory under the province of Syria. They now enter the tetrarchy of Philip, Herod Antipas's brother. Jesus is entering new territory: geographically and spiritually.

---

5. "the son of God, who is the end of the prophets" (Fox, *Works*, 7:43)

Our Example (Mark 8)

WHOM DO MEN SAY THAT I AM?

A sense of oneself can arise either from within or be derived from the opinion of others. Jesus is here asking for information on how he is seen, not solely to determine whether others see him accurately but also, perhaps, to propel him into accepting the work he is to do and the role he is to embody.

"One of the prophets" (28), his disciples reply. It is not enough. Prophets are sent to bear witness to the kingdom, but they do not reside in it;[6] prophets bear witness to the Light, but they are not the Light. The identity Jesus is to have is not one that merely bears witness to but, in fact, *is* the Light.[7] He is to become that which is born witness to: to be one with the Light. His identity—no longer tied to self-concept and certainly not to the opinion of others—is distinct from these worldly means of gaining self-knowledge.

> But whom say ye that I am? . . . And he began to teach them, that the Son of man must suffer many things (29 and 31).

These two verses, 29 and 31, show Jesus transitioning from being grounded in his personal self (using the personal pronoun "I" [29]) to his new way of being, in which he refers to himself in the third person, "the Son of man" (31). No longer defined by solitary personhood, he speaks of himself as representative and forerunner of the new way of being: the Son of man, the second Adam.

THOU ART THE CHRIST

Perhaps Jesus needed to hear some headlong rashness to push him forward into accepting what he knew for certain must come. And

---

6. For I say unto you, Among those that are born of women there is not a greater prophet than John the Baptist: but he that is least in the kingdom of God is greater than he (Luke 7:28).

7. There was a man sent from God, whose name was John. The same came for a witness, to bear witness of the Light, that all men through him might believe. He was not that Light, but was sent to bear witness of that Light (John 1:6–8).

Peter was just the man to provide it! "And Peter answereth and saith unto him, Thou art the Christ" (29). Jesus's routine command, "they should tell no man of him" (30), validates Peter's assertion, and—now confident—Peter again steps forward, takes Jesus aside, and "rebuke[s]" him (32) after he's heard the dire forecast of Jesus's suffering, rejection, and execution. This time, however, Peter's rashness has landed him on the wrong side, and he incurs Jesus's strong rebuke in return. The back-and-forth positioning of Peter in this exchange suggests a similar back-and-forth struggle that Jesus must have experienced inwardly as he grew to accept what was to come. The passage shows the different forces at work—God's will versus man's (i.e., Satan's [33])—and the inward strife of man who is coming to grips with the will of God.

> That the Son of man must suffer many things, and be rejected of the elders, and of the chief priests, and scribes, and be killed, and after three days rise again (31).

CONCLUSION

This chapter began with Jesus teaching the multitude and realizing that his manner of teaching, as well as his interactions with adversaries, disciples, and those in need of healing, were no longer sufficient. Having become aware of that fact, he took steps to accept the new work and role required of him. In this final passage of chapter 8, we see him having accepted all, and he is now ready to resume teaching the people.

> And when he had called the people unto him with his disciples also, he said unto them, Whosoever will come after me, let him deny himself, and take up his cross, and follow me (34).

In the final passage of chapter 8, Jesus distills the nature of the struggle that he has undergone and which others, too, must undergo: denial of self and taking up the cross. In the Scriptures and "in the flesh," Jesus is an example for us: showing us the human

Our Example (Mark 8)

who senses the need for a better way and moves forward in truth and is ultimately given to embody the Truth and the Life. To quote Nayler once again, we are "to be led in a way [we] know not," a way not our own but Christ-taught, Light-filled. In this passage, Jesus firmly places the responsibility upon each person to undergo the struggle to renounce one's worldly self and preoccupation and to turn one's open, empty soul inward to receive the glorious substance that is Christ, the Light Within.

> Christ in his people is the substance of all figures, types, and shadows, fulfilling them in them, and setting them free from them: but as he is held forth in the scripture letter without them, and in the flesh without them, he is their example or figure, which are both one, that the same things might be fulfilled in them that were in Christ Jesus.[8]

---

8. Fox, *Works*, 3:592–3.

Preparing the Disciples (Mark 9)

And he said unto them, Verily I say unto you, That there be some of them that stand here, which shall not taste of death, till they have seen the kingdom of God come with power.

IN CHAPTER 8, WE saw Jesus accepting his new role as Messiah, which then allowed him to call others to the same self-denial or taking up of the cross to which he himself had acceded. One might think the first verse of chapter 9 (quoted above) would be better placed in the preceding chapter, as it continues the scene begun a few verses earlier in 8:34. Chapter 9, however, features Jesus preparing for his earthly departure by educating his disciples to the end that they and others might come to see the kingdom of God. Thus, it is appropriate to have stated at the beginning of this chapter the intent of the work for which the disciples are being trained: that some may come to see "the kingdom of God come with power."[1]

This teaching chapter has two main lessons: (1) there is a new vision of life that is above and beyond worldly capacity to know, and (2) its ways and means are distinct from worldly ways and means, and they are taught by the Son of God.

---

1. The King James Version is used throughout this essay.

Preparing the Disciples (Mark 9)

THE TRANSFIGURATION

How better to impress upon the three leading disciples (Peter, James, and John) that there is a reality hitherto beyond their ken than to bring them into a new space, "an high mountain" (2), and before their eyes to be moved into that brilliant reality, which is the Light! That this phenomenon is legitimately grounded in the tradition is affirmed by the appearance of Moses (the Law) and Elias (the Prophets). The disciples are desirous to normalize the event by building tabernacles, yet they are prevented from doing so. That is to say, they are prevented from taking an active hand in worship—worshiping in man's will—and are instead instructed by God to worship in the new way: by hearing the Light that is the Son of God (7). Having witnessed the transfiguration from flesh to Light is the first and necessary lesson for these disciples, for until then, only the darkness of worldly life had suffused their awareness. They had need to see, to experience the Light, for how could they bring others into the kingdom if they themselves did not know, had not seen, its reality.

In admonishing the disciples to "tell no man what things they had seen" (9), Jesus is taking steps to prevent speculation. It is essential that knowledge be gained in a manner more akin to sensory experience, i.e., hearing, seeing, tasting rather than conjecture. For human pride often enthrones conjecture with a certainty that is not warranted and thus usurps Truth's rightful place.

It is conjecture about the meaning of "rising from the dead" that the three disciples engage in amongst themselves as they come down the mountain (10). That they then question Jesus about the prophet Elias tells of the tradition's close association of Elias's return—a prophet rising from the dead—with the subsequent coming of the Lord.[2] Jesus identifies John the Baptist with Elias, in that the righteousness of which man is capable in and of himself was the necessary and core attribute of all prophets, and

---

2. "Behold, I will send you Elijah the prophet before the coming of the Lord" (Mal 4:5). "Elijah" is the prophet's name in the Hebrew language, while "Elias" is the Greek form.

John exemplified this quality most fully. Ironically, in chapter 6, these several ideas of rising from the dead regarding Elias, John the Baptist, and Jesus are likewise linked by Herod, John's executioner.[3] In turn, Jesus obliquely links Elias, John, and Herod in the verse concluding this section: "But I say unto you, That Elias is indeed come, and they have done unto him whatsoever they listed as it is written of him" (13). That the messianic rising follows upon the prophetic diminishment is a motif presented repeatedly in this and the previous chapter where Jesus himself moved from one to the other: we are being told that the prophetic and the messianic are linked and similar but sufficiently distinct to have their difference noted repeatedly at various times and by disparate characters.

In this first lesson given to Jesus's disciples, the reality of the kingdom of God is shown in the transfiguration (2–3) where flesh becomes Light and the beloved Son is to be heard (7). Furthermore, the triumphant reign over inevitable worldly opposition is foreshadowed in the words "the Son of man were risen from the dead" (9). Having experienced the Light of Christ and having been taught the dynamics of opposition and triumph that are to be expected, the disciples are now ready to see a demonstration of the work they will do. They are to see humanity in its rebellion, its ignorance, pride, cruelty, helplessness, and grief, and they are to overcome it all.

THE PEOPLE AND THE AUTHORITIES (14-16)

Increasingly, Jesus has become less willing to engage the authorities: in verse 16, he asks a question of them and does not stay to hear their answer. It would appear that his previous encounters with the authorities were predicated upon weaning the people away from their influence. That is no longer necessary, as the people who have

---

3. And king Herod heard of him [Jesus] . . . and he said, That John the Baptist was risen from the dead, and therefore mighty works do shew forth themselves in him. Others said, That it is Elias. . . . But when Herod heard thereof, he said, It is John, whom I beheaded: he is risen from the dead (Mark 6:14–16).

been speaking with the scribes quickly lose interest in them when Jesus appears (15). Diverting his attention from the scribes and moving on to those conscious of the need for help, Jesus models spiritual triage: a lesson in practicality for his disciples. Time and resources are limited and must be spent where most productive.

THE HEALING (17-29)

Although this healing story features particular characters, a distraught father and his demon-possessed son, it serves, in fact, as a universal template for humanity's unredeemed condition. In Scripture healing stories, a son or daughter—that which is most precious to us in our fleshly life—often functions as a symbol for the soul—that which is most precious to us in our spiritual life. That the son in this story is debilitated by a troubling spirit is to say that the human soul is troubled by a debilitating spirit. Upon hearing the father's list of his son's symptoms, Jesus immediately interjects the diagnosis: "O faithless generation" (19). Note his use of the word "generation"; he does not address the man directly but expands his particular problem to encompass many people: an indication that it is lack of faith that universally troubles and debilitates the human soul, the human life.

The father, brought to desperation in his fully exercised but inadequate power, cries out in tears from his earnest heart, "Lord, I believe; help thou mine unbelief" (24). All the elements for receiving faith are thus present: the recognition of the soul's need, that all one's earnest effort cannot meet that need, and the crying out for help. The Lord can then proceed to exorcise the demonic spirit from the soul and forever prevent its return (25). The son's appearing dead at first but then lifted up to life (27) prefigures the resurrection to life that Jesus will model following his crucifixion and entombment, which he refers to a few verses later (31). His crucifixion, entombment, and resurrection, in turn, prefigures our inward, spiritual ascension to Life.

This healing episode is a lesson that provides a prototype for the work the disciples must come to do. We are reminded that it has been a lesson when they ask Jesus why they themselves could not cast out the demon (28). He replies, "This kind can come forth by nothing, but by prayer and fasting" (29). Fasting is the restriction of worldly appetite, and prayer is communion with God. Jesus is teaching his disciples that the demonic is cast out following the restriction of the worldly appetite and the ascension into heavenly communion.

HOW THE DISCIPLES ARE TO CONDUCT THEMSELVES

Having shown the disciples the work they are to do in the world, Jesus then spends the remainder of this chapter on the inward discipline they are to maintain that they may perform this work, both individually and among themselves. Each disciple must consider his primary role to be serving others in their progress toward the kingdom (35); it is the kingdom that matters, not one's position in the worldly hierarchy. To empathize with and assist the unworldly innocent is to integrate oneself into the way of Christ and God (37). Attend to the spirit a person manifests, not to the letter of his words (39–40). Those who provide relief to you (and you will need it!) shall be favored by God, and, conversely, for those who thwart the unworldly innocent, it were better for them to be without life altogether, for their souls are irrevocably sunk in the chaos of hell (42).

> And if thy hand offend thee, cut it off: it is better for thee to enter into life maimed, than having two hands to go into hell, into the fire that never shall be quenched: Where their worm dieth not, and the fire is not quenched. And if thy foot offend thee, cut it off: it is better for thee to enter halt into life, than having two feet to be cast in hell, into the fire that never shall be quenched: Where their worm dieth not, and the fire is not quenched. And if thine eye offend thee, pluck it out: it is better for thee to enter into the kingdom of God with one eye, than having two eyes to be cast into hell fire: Where their worm dieth not, and the fire is not quenched (43–48).

Preparing the Disciples (Mark 9)

This passage near the end of chapter 9 differs in style from what has come before; through its poetry, the passage indelibly stresses the necessity of disallowing worldly inclinations from interfering with one's determination to enter the kingdom. For if a person does not enter the kingdom himself, he hardly can expect to assist others in the same pursuit. What one does (the hand), where one goes (the foot), what one desires (the eye) are to be kept aligned and purposeful to the end that the kingdom is entered. Maintaining this intent is essential, and so Jesus uses repetition and refrain to impress upon his disciples the all-important oversight and regulation of their inward state.

> For every one shall be salted with fire, and every sacrifice shall be salted with salt. Salt is good, but if the salt have lost his saltness, wherewith will ye season it? (49–50)

Beautiful is Jesus's play upon the word "salt" in the final two verses of this chapter. Continuing with the reference to the "fire" of hell from the previous admonitory passage, he speaks of the difficulty of making the sacrifice of one's worldly self (everyone is "salted with fire") while also alluding to the tradition's practice of the salting of temple sacrifices.[4] "Salt is good"; it is the essential seasoning: just as a vital soul seasons all one's being. Life loses its palatability when not seasoned with a soul that lives in the Light. Jesus completes this teaching chapter by calling his disciples to keep this necessary seasoning, the living soul, in themselves, for it is that which allows for "peace one with another" (50).

Throughout this teaching chapter, Jesus has provided experiential knowledge of the kingdom, a demonstration of the work to be done, and numerous guidelines for maintaining the vitality of spiritual life within and among his disciples.

---

4. And every oblation of thy meat offering shalt thou season with salt; neither shalt thou suffer the salt of the covenant of thy God to be lacking from thy meat offering: with all thine offerings thou shalt offer salt (Lev 2:13).

Meaning in Life (Mark 10)

[T]he lack of meaning in life is a soul-sickness whose full extent and import our age has not yet begun to comprehend.
—Carl Jung

Today on my walk around the Philadelphia neighborhood where I live, I noticed several small garden sculptures: a trumpeting elephant made of stone; a butterfly fashioned from iron; a displaced fountain *putto*, also of stone; and, at the base of an old oak, a conclave of gnomes! It occurred to me that raw materials—such as stone, iron, and plaster—when given recognizable form, take on meaning, not only for the maker but also for the viewer. The fashioned shape elicits associations, calling to mind earlier events or periods in one's life. It may provide a connection between past and present, enhancing one's own unique life narrative. Thus, the form or image calls forth some sense of personal meaning. These garden ornaments did so in a minor, trivial way; nevertheless, they provided evidence that the need for and pursuit of meaning is a strong motive for us humans, one that animates our lives.

That the desire for and pursuit of meaning must be rightly ordered is the primary theme of Mark 10. When wrongly directed, this pursuit can lessen life's quality and blunt its purpose. Chapter 10 presents our hero, Jesus, thwarting the idolatrous desires of

SOCIAL DOMINANCE (1-9)

The first interchange in this chapter is with the Pharisees (2). This group assumes that their expert knowledge of their nation's history, the Law of Moses, and the tradition of the elders entitles them to a position of authority within their society. Jesus has threatened their assumption and their social position by drawing the interest and admiration of the people away from them and to himself. Through their expertise, the Pharisees seek to retain their superior social status, which wrongfully gives meaning to their lives. Their intent in approaching Jesus in the beginning story of this chapter is to diminish him by showing that he's out of keeping with the tradition (thereby alienating those who flock to his teaching). They present Jesus with a question, which if answered either yes or no would ensure their authority and dominance.

Their question was "Is it lawful for a man to put away his wife?"[5] For Jesus to answer yes would have signaled submission to the Law's authority as well as to the Pharisees themselves whose expertise was knowledge of the Law; to answer no would have put Jesus at variance with Moses and the tradition, thus invalidating him with the people. Either answer would have put the Pharisees in a position of social dominance through authoritative knowledge. Jesus's answer ("For the hardness of your heart [Moses] wrote you this precept" [5]) skirts their trap by placing the necessity for the precept upon the people's shortcomings, for which Moses wisely made allowance. Thus, Jesus doesn't discredit himself by denying Moses and the tradition but allies himself with them, while still noting the precept's drawback. His superior grasp of the tradition then allows him to pronounce the earlier, holy intent of marriage: "Therefore shall man leave his father and his mother, and shall cleave unto his wife: and they shall be one flesh" (Gen 2:24

---

5. Epigraph. "Lack of Religion," 0:39. The King James Version (KJV) and the New English Bible (NEB) are used in this essay.

[KJV]). He points to the prelapsarian perfect intent of God, while the Pharisees can offer up only a stop-gap rule for inhibiting the debasement of Fallen humanity. Showing his unity with the Source of the tradition, Jesus disrupts the Pharisees' idolatrous intent to generate meaning through social dominance that is based upon scholarly expertise.

SOCIAL ATTACHMENT (10-12)

Keeping to the same topic of marriage when he is alone with his disciples (10-12), Jesus dislodges a different error: that life's meaning is found in having the "right" partner or spouse. This belief often leads to one spouse divorcing the other in order to marry again: behavior that Jesus condemns. Interesting to note, it is not leaving the spouse that is condemned, for he sanctions that act when done "for [his] sake, and the gospel's" (29 [KJV]). To leave the spouse, however, in order to "marry another" (11 [KJV]) is to believe that one's well-being depends upon having the right spouse. There are good marriages and there are bad, but neither can the good ones excel, nor the bad ones disrupt the essential, primary relationship with Christ Within (another way of saying being within the kingdom of God) wherein true meaning and thus well-being are both found.

Jesus has now confuted two prominent forms of misplaced meaning (idolatry), both concerned with social relationships: (1) dominance over or (2) attachment to others. Neither yields the meaning we are to find.

THE KINGDOM

As though to present a corrective to the Pharisees' grab for social dominance and the misguided estimation of spousal attachment, the narrative turns to a short episode in which Jesus responds to young children (13-16). A young child longs for what it wants without considering barriers, costs, or conflicts. He hasn't yet developed the ability to weigh, calculate, deliberate upon, postpone, or sublimate his desire: he simply wants what he wants, now and wholeheartedly. When this pure, simple condition of longing for the kingdom of God is known within (Matt 6:22), entry is provided, to both the Giver's and the given's delight.

RICHES (17-25)

Riches provide many kinds of power: opportunity, security, comfort, luxury, status, esteem, and influence are some. The numerous material and social goods that riches can provide have always made life more amenable in the many cultures of this world, and therein, acquisition and retention of wealth has widely figured as preeminently meaningful. Many have given over their lives to its pursuit. The man who "came running, and kneeled to [Jesus]," though wealthy, would add "eternal life" to his list of life-enhancing possessions (17). Jesus's first words to him, however, hint that the man needs to discern and prioritize: he states, "[T]here is none good but *one*" (18 [KJV]). He again emphasizes singularity when he says, "*One* thing you lack" (21 [NEB]). [Italics are mine.] Jesus is leading the man to realize eternal life is the one essential, and not an item to be grouped with the many worldly possessions already in hand. Eternal life is a separate category of its own:[6] it is the unique, original Substance, next to which great wealth, with all its advantages, is insignificant and can be relinquished.

Alone again with his disciples, Jesus lists the possessions and relationships in which humanity is prone to place life's meaning, and he states their combined worth is not to be compared to the one essential that excels them all: eternal life (29-30). To show the

---

6. That "eternal life" is in a separate category apart from worldly goods is indicated by the phrase that precedes and separates it from the list: that is, "and in the world to come" (30 [KJV]). This phrase does not refer to a state to be known following the death of the body, as traditions other than Quaker would have it. Rather it refers to that state in which, having received inward knowledge of God—the Light of Christ—the recipient's worldview is changed so dramatically that he appears to have entered a different world. That is the "world to come" to which Jesus refers in verse 30.

error of placing meaning in the accumulation of worldly goods, Jesus offers the maxim "But many that are first shall be last; and the last first" (31 [KJV]). To be "first" in the world requires adopting cultural values and devoting life's substance to their attainment; whereas to seek and find the kingdom, eternal life, is to receive from God a personal sense of meaning that is beyond that which the world has to offer (30).

PERSECUTION (30-34)

Nestled within the list of abundance promised to those who forfeit worldly pursuits for the sake of the gospel is a sharp spike of warning: "[they] shall receive . . . persecutions" (30 [KJV]). Jesus expands upon this warning to his disciples on their walk toward Jerusalem, detailing the assault upon his dignity and person that will occur there. It will be an attack upon his power to sustain himself in the world; his human vulnerability is to be thoroughly exposed and compromised in every way: he is to be humiliated, mocked, scourged, and spat upon,[7] and he is to be killed (34).

Jesus's work is to present the way we humans are to gain meaning that withstands and overcomes the humiliation of being vulnerable creatures, driven by fear and desire. His teaching contradicts the ways and means by which societies fabricate meaning by lessening the mental impact of vulnerability and mortality. These societal ways simulate true, personal meaning in that they make tolerable the intolerable consciousness of weakness, temporality, and inevitable death. Jesus attacks these false formulations of meaning that man has imaged, constructed, and subjected himself

---

7. "Humiliate" comes from its Latin root "humus," meaning earth or ground. To be humiliated is figuratively to be returned to the ground: to be put in mind of our mortality, our vulnerability. Note that Jesus ends this description of his humiliation with the words "and the third day he shall rise again" (34). This rising again affirms the superiority of the Way that he teaches and performs over the worldly way of attempting to gain meaning through elevating oneself over others. The rising from the dead (from the earth) seems impossible to the worldly, but those who have been raised to know eternal life can testify to its reality, as Jesus does at the end of verse 34.

to in worship. They hobble man in his short spell of time upon the earth by waylaying and dulling the anxiety of having been created mortal: his anxious awareness that he, the man of sin,[8] is not the uncreated, eternal God.

EXERCISING AUTHORITY (35-45)

This chapter began with the Pharisees bid to gain social dominance, and, as if to show the stranglehold this particular idolatry has on humanity, the problem again presents itself: now within the small circle of disciples. The sons of Zebedee seek social status and authority: to sit one on each side of their leader "in [his] glory" (37 [KJV]), and the other disciples resent the two brothers' request for privileged status (41). Unlike in the earlier confrontation with the Pharisees, Jesus here finds it worthwhile to explain rightly ordered social interaction. After acknowledging the worldly (Gentile [42]) way of hierarchical exercise of power, he explains the new order, which is its inverse: "whosoever will be great among you, shall be your minister" (43 [KJV]), and then applies the maxim to himself (45).

THE HEALING (46-52)

In both the previous and final passages of this chapter, Jesus has asked petitioners what they would have him do for them (36, 51). The sons of Zebedee sought worldly gain in exalted social position, and they were denied. The blind beggar asked to receive his sight. Bartimaeus knows he's blind; knows he's a dependent beggar; knows Jesus is the son of David (the Messiah); and deeply, simply longs for wholeness. Though bullied (48), he refuses to be silenced, mollified, or co-opted. He continues to cry out for mercy: for sight, for wholeness, for well-being.

---

8. "the man of sin . . . [w]ho opposeth and exalteth himself above all that is called God . . . so that he as God sitteth in the temple of God, shewing himself that he is God" (2 Thess 2:3-4).

Bartimaeus's admission of need exhibited his faith in the truth. It is this faith that made him whole: "Go thy way; thy faith hath made thee whole" (52 [KJV]). In seeing the truth of his condition; casting away the garment that covered him (50), that symbol of worldly goods and aspiration; and rising in response to being called (50), Bartimaeus expressed faith that the Creator intends goodness and truth for his creatures, for Creation. All who have been made whole through the same excruciating process know that to "[g]o thy way" (as Jesus commands the now-sighted) is to continue, as did Bartimaeus, to follow Jesus. "And immediately he received his sight, and followed Jesus in the way" (52 [KJV]).[9]

Longtime suffering awareness ("soul-sickness") would teach us that we ourselves cannot heal our inward ills. Idolatry is humanity's attempt to do so. Human beings cannot construct for themselves authentic meaning, in which all the divergent aspects of the self coherently integrate and rest upon a single, solid foundation, resulting in felt wholeness and peace. Truly meaningful life is gained only when the Light of Christ enters and integrates one's being by means of his singular power and glory.

---

9. To "follow" or imitate "Jesus in the way" does not mean to use as one's primary guide the words he spoke and the acts he performed while he walked upon the earth. Rather the phrase should be interpreted "in a deeper sense," as Jung does in his book *Alchemical Studies*: "The imitation of Christ might well be understood in a deeper sense. It could be taken as the duty to realize one's deepest conviction with the same courage and the same self-sacrifice shown by Jesus" ("Lack of Religion," 10:00). I would add that for the Christian, the "deepest conviction" is found in coming into unity with Christ Within.

The Subsidiary Flesh (Mark 11)

"Whatsoever is excellent, whatsoever is noble, whatsoever is worthy, whatsoever is desirable" in the Christian faith, is ascribed to this *Spirit*, without which it could no more subsist than the outward world without the sun. Hereunto have all true Christians, in all ages, attributed their strength and life. It is by this Spirit that they avouch themselves to have been converted to God, to have been redeemed from the world, to have been strengthened in their weakness, comforted in their afflictions, confirmed in their temptations, emboldened in their sufferings, and triumphed in the midst of all their persecutions. Yea, the writings of all true Christians are full of the great and notable things which they all affirm themselves to have done, by the power, and virtue, and efficacy of the Spirit of God working in them.

—ROBERT BARCLAY

IN THIS EXCERPT FROM the Second Proposition of the *Apology*,[1] Barclay distinguishes between the Spirit itself and those in whom it is revealed or received. In being given this Spirit's power and goodness, "true Christians" are thereby enabled to act with "strength and life." Seventeenth-century Friends saw that the Spirit was a distinct, enabling power that superseded whatever virtues and values they had chosen to adopt for themselves in their reliance

1. Barclay, *Apology*, 42–43.

upon their natural powers of reason and conscience. Chapter 11 in the Book of Mark aims to clarify the difference between the Spirit and the flesh, the flesh being all that figures into natural human capacity in and of itself: including thinking, feeling, and sensing.

The previous chapter in Mark taught that we human beings are prone to assigning life's meaning to that which is attainable by and through our own fleshly nature and that this is the error of idolatry and a misuse of the gift of life. In this chapter, Spirit and flesh are metaphorically and repeatedly distinguished one from the other, always with the intent to show the flesh is to be subsidiary and attendant to the quickening Spirit. The function of the flesh is to assist, carry, and house a Spirit distinct from itself: that is, the flesh is to assist, carry, and house the Spirit of God.

THE COLT

> [Y]e shall find a colt tied, whereon never man sat; loose him, and bring him (2).

At the beginning of chapter 11, we are immediately launched into a metaphor that illustrates the difference between the Spirit of God and fleshly human nature. The donkey, a beast of burden, is commandeered to bear "the Lord [who] hath need of him" (3): just as the human being, in all that comprises his nature, is called to bear the Spirit of God. Human nature is distinct from this Spirit but is to carry and serve it as the donkey is to carry and serve the Lord.

In commentaries on this passage, much is made of the Messianic prophecy in Zechariah 9:9.[2] What interests me about the link between the two passages, however, is not that the Mark passage confirms Jesus as the Messiah whom prophets anticipated, but that the lowliness of the animal is emphasized. Not only is the Lord and King's transport a donkey but even less than a donkey: it is

---

2. "Rejoice greatly, O daughter of Zion; shout, O daughter of Jerusalem: behold, thy King cometh unto thee: he is just, and having salvation; lowly and riding upon an ass, and upon a colt the foal of an ass" (Zech 9:9). The King James Version of the Bible was used throughout this essay.

The Subsidiary Flesh (Mark 11)

a donkey colt, not even a fully grown animal. This detail suggests that that which carries the Lord is a creature not fully matured, not fully realized, which is to say, in his fleshly nature, unredeemed man is the not-fully-realized Creation.

Historically, the animal on which a person rode indicated his nature or status. (And this has carried over even into our own day in the type of car one drives!) The emphasis on the lowliness of the animal that transports Jesus—not simply a donkey but a donkey colt—augments the contrast between the creaturely flesh and that which it is called to carry: "thy King" (Zech 9:9), "the Lord" (Mark 11:3).

That the donkey is one upon which "never man sat" (2) suggests the newness and forward movement in the human endeavor that Jesus's ride into Jerusalem signals, sometimes called the "Messianic Age." Never before has the (fleshly) creature been loosed and brought into the service of the One who commandeers him. Well do onlookers cast their garments and branches—worldly possessions and nature—and shout "Hosanna" to the One "that cometh in the name [power] of the Lord" (8–9). It is a new era in which humanity may now enter into holiness "[b]y the new and living way which he hath consecrated for us, through the veil, that is to say, his flesh" (Heb 10:20). The "forerunner" (6:20) is to bridle the fleshly nature that he—and thus, by implication, all humankind—may carry and serve the living God.

THE TEMPLE AND THE FIG TREE (11–21)

The next eleven verses in this chapter weave together two strands of metaphor, each conveying in its own way the distinction between flesh and Spirit. The two metaphors are interlaced as are the two locations in which they occur: Jerusalem and Bethany (the road from Bethany). That the two metaphors are to be considered variations of the same idea is set out in verse 11, which has no substantial content other than to establish there are two locations—and two incidents—where the flesh has failed to serve the Spirit. That there are two incidents to describe this failure rather than the single success shown earlier with the colt suggests failure is prevalent. The two strands of this passage—the defiled temple and the barren fig tree—illustrate this disorder or failure through metaphor.

In Jerusalem, the defiled temple does not house the activity of prayer but has become a place to buy and sell (15) and a throughway for other concerns (16). The temple is a building where the Spirit is to be housed, just as the creaturely flesh is to house the Spirit. To misappropriate one's life to secure worldly, fleshly gain is to make the temple of the Lord—to make of oneself—a thief-inhabited den (17).

Secondly, the fig tree's primary function is to produce fruit, just as human beings when rightly ordered will produce fruits of the Spirit. The tree—or flesh—that produces nothing of value to the Lord, no fruit but only leaves, is cursed to be eternally without true purpose or meaning: "No man eat fruit of thee hereafter for ever" (14). Absent his true purpose and meaning, the human being withers away, as does this fig tree (21).

FAITH (22-26)

Up to this point in the chapter, we have been given one illustration of rightly ordered flesh bearing the commanding Spirit (the colt bearing the Lord), as well as two intertwined examples of fleshly failure to house or bear that Spirit (the defiled temple and the barren fig tree): failures that Jesus condemned by violent act and word (14-17). The short sermon that follows these illustrations contains Jesus's admonition and guidance for making the changeover from the fleshly nature to a Spirit-led state, where the Spirit of God is manifested through the flesh. It is a condition called by many names: "second birth"; "incarnation"; "the kingdom of heaven"; "Christ Within"; "Way"; "Truth"; "Life"; or simply, as in this passage, "faith."

> Have faith in God. For verily I say unto you. That whosoever shall say unto this mountain, Be thou removed, and be thou cast into the sea; and shall not doubt in his

The Subsidiary Flesh (Mark 11)

heart, but shall believe that those things which he saith shall come to pass; he shall have whatsoever he saith. Therefore I say unto you, what things soever ye desire, when ye pray, believe that ye receive them, and ye shall have them (22–24).

A mountain cast into the sea at the behest of one who wholeheartedly believes his words ensure the event will happen is figurative language. It is an imaginative way of saying that through faith we experience our human nature transcended: we enter prayer by calling the mountainous ego to be set aside, having no doubt Christ will appear to replace our now absent self-centeredness with his own commanding presence. Confident expectation, Jesus teaches here, is the right frame of mind for entering into prayerful communion with God.

A literal interpretation of verses 22–24 could arise only in a fleshly mind, a mind in which Scriptures' miracles do not recall inward experience but instead are used to violate reason and also, as a consequence, conscience. (Cognitive dissonance goes unchecked in minds not given to truth.) Heavenly gifts of reason and conscience are violated when one compels oneself to believe literally that a mountain could be cast into the sea at one's behest. (Furthermore, Jesus reminds us elsewhere of the limits to our natural powers.)[3] The reasoning of the flesh is inadequate to interpret miracles in Scripture, which are experientially understood by those who have known the Spirit's visitation.[4]

---

3. Neither shalt thou swear by thy head, because thou canst not make one hair white or black (Matt 5:36).

4. Another common error of the fleshly mind is its denouncing the flesh (usually meaning the body or the intellect) as being opposed to God. The intellect and the body are gifts from God and as such are not evil; it is their idolatrous misuse that is wrong. To understand this fallacy, consider this analogy: a hammer is a tool that is intended for use in construction; that it can also be used destructively as a weapon does not make the hammer in itself evil. The rightly used intellect is likewise a tool that constructively carries, assists, and houses (gives expression to) the Spirit of truth. Wrongly used, the intellect corruptly turns from the authority of the Spirit of truth and instead acts out its rebellion by destructively trafficking in lies and confusion, that its chosen idol might be served. Chapter 11 teaches flesh must be subsidiary to the Spirit, and

> What things soever ye desire, when ye pray, believe that
> ye receive them, and ye shall have them (24).

How easily the fleshly mind can make verse 24 a genie-in-a-lamp situation! One does not petition God for worldly goods or power. When flesh is rightly ordered, we pray to receive God's Spirit, which is of supreme value beyond all fleshly accommodation. This is the primary lesson that Jesus's acceptance of the cross teaches: the mountainous, fleshly nature is settled low or cast aside and the Spirit received, as it is known and believed in.

In the final two verses of this short sermon, Jesus offers us a kind of litmus test to discern whether one is oriented to the flesh or to the Spirit:

> And when ye stand praying, forgive, if ye have ought against any: that your Father also which is in heaven may forgive you your trespasses. But if ye do not forgive, neither will your Father which is in heaven forgive your trespasses (25–26).

The passage of time can lessen the pain of having been victimized, yet judgment and contempt may linger on, taking their toll upon the soul. Forgiveness is a gift from God that accompanies entry into the inward state where worldly advantage or deprivation do not figure, and we judge not at all: neither self nor others. (Yet, any judgment of self or others given therein is right judgment [John 8:15–16].) In that inward state, one bears no ill will toward those who have trespassed, as our well-being is as inviolate as the One who presides within. It is only when faith has been bestowed upon us that dark resentment for harm done disappears, subsumed in the brightness of his glory. To attempt to forgive without heavenly power is like jumping from the earth and expecting to remain airborne. The gravity of our Fallen estate does not allow it.

---

therein is it of good service to God. Truth (Spirit) manifesting in and through the intellect (flesh) is the prophets' way of bringing heaven to earth. The "Word made flesh" (John 1:14) is a phrase that tells of the essential, necessary role flesh has to play in God's Providence.

The Subsidiary Flesh (Mark 11)

That both admonitions—to have faith and to forgive—are presented as though it were a person's choice to have or do either of them functions to direct the person toward these goals. He is to do his utmost to regulate himself that he may be prepared to receive these heavenly gifts. The flesh is to be directed toward virtue and truth, but of itself, the flesh can do no more.

AUTHORITY (27-33)

In the time since Jesus's disruption of idolatrous activity in the temple (15–16), the scribes and chief priests have been conniving to "destroy" him, for he has amazed the people with his powerful teaching (18). As is typical of these religious leaders, they come to Jesus with prepared trick questions: "By what authority doest thou these things? and who gave thee this authority to do these things?" (29) These questions continue the chapter's theme of distinguishing between two forces known within—the Spirit which commands and empowers (the authority), and the flesh which assists, carries, or houses that Spirit. The leaders are challenging Jesus to name the Spirit, or authority, that he carries within.

Any direct response to the leaders' questions would station that cohort as the authority that must be answered. Furthermore, in answering their questions, Jesus would open the issue to argument and refutation, thus elevating the priests in people's eyes through Jesus's willingness to engage them. Jesus neither answers their question directly, nor allows them the opportunity to refute or argue. He instead puts them back on their heels by asking, in turn, an unanswerable question: "The baptism of John, was it from heaven, or of men?" And he caps his authoritative stance with an imperative: "answer me" (30).

Though the question is about John the Baptist, Jesus holds the like esteem of the people as well as the antipathy of the priests, so any answer the priests give regarding John will, to the people, apply equally to Jesus. Thus Jesus turns the tables on the priests by compelling *them* to answer the same question they have asked and he has refused to answer. This they cannot do and still maintain their authority with the people. Privy to their reasoning, we see that truth figures not one whit; high social position is uppermost in their calculations. This firmly categorizes these leaders as idolators, who corrupt themselves by instrumental use of speech in service to their fleshly will:

> And they reasoned with themselves, saying, If we shall say, From heaven; he will say, Why then did ye not believe him? But if we shall say, Of men, they feared the people: for all men counted John, that he was a prophet indeed (31–32).

Chapter 11 has taught that flesh and Spirit are two distinct powers and that the flesh is to be subsidiary to the commanding authority of Spirit. In the final passage of this chapter, we saw these two powers—flesh and Spirit—come face to face, contesting which had the upper hand. The religious leaders, in practice, regarded the flesh to be the authority they serve, having made for themselves an idol of their position within society. They have corrupted the right order of Spirit commanding flesh and instead made flesh its own purpose and rule. Jesus refused to give way to the imposition of their corruption: his defiance is evident throughout the exchange. He vanquished these contenders, therein demonstrating the true power and authority of the Spirit of God that he carries within and, through his flesh, has manifested. In Jesus's final statement, we see the same distinction made that has imbued this chapter from start to finish: the distinction between the subsidiary, manifesting flesh (the "I") and the animating authority of the Spirit of God. "Neither do I tell you by what authority I do these things" (33).

The Lesson of the Fig Tree
(11:12–14, 20–22)

THE FOLLOWING IS BASED upon gospel ministry given in a Philadelphia meeting on May 6, 2018.

There is a story of Jesus and his disciples walking toward Jerusalem. Along the way, Jesus saw a fig tree in the distance, and upon approaching it, he saw that it had leaves but no fruit, "for the time of the figs was not yet" (13). Then Jesus cursed the tree, saying, "No man eat fruit of thee hereafter for ever" (14).[1] Though it was the nature of the tree to bear figs only in season, he cursed the tree for having no fruit.

As with so many incidents that take place in Scripture, this story tells us something of ourselves, and in this story, we are being taught something about what is expected of us as human beings. Like the fig tree, we humans have a particular nature, the human nature, and what its fruits are is well-known to each of us: we have our particular strengths and limitations, our seasons of fear and desire, our fruits of virtue and vice. These all are a part of our human nature.

We are being told in this story that just as more was expected of the fig tree than its nature could yield, more, too, is expected of us than that which our nature can produce. To meet the expectations that are placed upon us—and that we place upon ourselves—we

---

1. The King James Version is used throughout the essay.

must be more than what our nature confines us to be. We are commanded to be righteous and loving (John 15:12), yet human nature does not allow us to be this; it always lets us down. We try and we fail, and we try again.

How are we to handle this problem with which we are cursed? Is self-deceit our nature's only possible escape from imposed and internalized expectations of the unattainable? Is the honest person's only option the agonized cry of Paul: "O wretched man that I am! Who shall deliver me from the body of this death?" (Rom 7:24)

It is through receiving the spirit of Christ that we become more than our nature allows. It is through receiving this Spirit that we may bear divine fruit of love and righteousness, which is beyond human nature to yield. We prepare to receive this divine Spirit by stilling our human nature and waiting in truth, in that emptiness where, in truth, Truth is not yet come. Through waiting to receive, Friends found that Truth is given, and our human nature transcended and fulfilled. Friends of Truth discovered that we could come into unity with the One whose divine image we bear as sons and daughters of God, and thus come into loving, righteous fellowship with one another. Their discovery confirms the reality that, in any age, we humans can bear the fruits of the Spirit, in season and out, no longer prevented by the confines of our nature; it is the one true miracle!

> Who are ingrafted into Christ? Can any one be ingrafted into him, but as he is inwardly revealed and made known? Yea, is not he in them who are ingrafted into him, and are not they in him? Is not he that is truly regenerated cut off from the old stock within, from the root of bitterness within; and is not he implanted into the new stock within also; insomuch as he sensibly feeleth the pure, holy root of life bear him, and the sap thereof springing up in him, causing him to bring forth fruit to God in due season?
> —Isaac Penington[2]

---

2. Penington, *Works*, 4:165.

The Practice of Religion (Mark 12)

And the Lord God of their fathers sent to them by his messengers, rising up betimes, and sending; because he had compassion on his people, and on his dwelling place: But they mocked the messengers of God, and despised his words, and misused his prophets, until the wrath of the Lord arose against his people, till there was no remedy.

2 Chr 36:15–16

IN CHAPTER 12 OF Mark's Gospel, Jesus stands in the Father's authority and counsel against an onslaught of religious and political factions that resent his influence with the people. His strength arises from the Almighty; mere fleshly will succumbs in his Presence. We readers need to see this utter rout, to see Jesus run circles around his adversaries, for the events that shortly will come to pass would tell of defeat and death at the hands of "the rulers of darkness of this world."[1] The chief priests, scribes, and elders; the Pharisees and the Herodians; and the Sadducees all approach Jesus with deceit and lust for power defiling their hearts and mouths. Jesus sees and exposes the specific errors that characterize each group.

---

1. Eph 6:12 (The King James Version is used except where otherwise noted where The New English Bible is used.)

A QUAKER READING OF MARK'S GOSPEL

PRIESTS, ELDERS, AND SCRIBES (1–12)

> [H]e sent him also last unto them, saying, They will reverence my son (6).

Chapter 11 ended with Jesus's refusal to give the chief priests, scribes, and elders an answer to their demand to name the authority by which he acts. In the first nine verses of chapter 12, he answers this question in a roundabout way: by presenting these religious leaders with a parable. In this parable, the owner, builder, and lord of the vineyard (1) is God; the tenants or managers to whom he has rented the vineyard (1) are the chief priests, scribes, and elders; the servants sent to gather the fruits of the vineyard (2–5) are the prophets; and "his own dear son" (6 [NEB]) is Jesus himself. Jesus has not only conveyed that he, as son, acts upon his Father's authority but that these religious leaders oppose that authority, and, consequently, "the lord of the vineyard" (9 [KJV]) will destroy them and give their position of privilege and responsibility to others.

> But the tenants said to one another, "This is the heir; come on, let us kill him, and the property will be ours." So they seized him and killed him, and flung his body out of the vineyard. What will the owner of the vineyard do? He will come and put the tenants to death and give the vineyard to others (7–9 [NEB]).

Jesus adds to this damning parable by quoting verses from a psalm,[2] which squarely puts him in line with the tradition, thereby dislodging these religious leaders from their alleged stronghold. He completes the drubbing by attributing all to "the Lord's doing," depicting himself simply as an astonished onlooker: "This was the Lord's doing and it is marvellous in our eyes" (11). That he presents himself as an observer rather than the proprietor of his words tells us that throughout this lengthy monologue (1–11), he has never

---

2. "And have ye not read this scripture; The stone which the builders rejected is become the head of the corner: This was the Lord's doing and it is marvellous in our eyes" (10–11). Jesus is quoting Psalm 118, verses 22 and 23.

The Practice of Religion (Mark 12)

lost sight of this group's initial challenge to name the authority by which he acts: it is "the Lord's doing," not his own. His intelligence is dizzyingly brilliant and is itself proof of his reliance upon divine power and authority.

The scribes, whom he addresses in this parable, were those whose profession was to know the Law. This work required a scholarly intelligence: one that is agile and diligent in recollection, analysis, and research. The intelligence that Jesus manifests is not scholarly; it is instead grounded in the Source of intelligence and as such, surpasses all delimited expressions of that power: scholarly, sensory, social, technical, or creative intelligence.

Scholars, such as the scribes, have tried throughout history to put themselves forward in matters of spiritual discernment, not grasping that revelation given through the prophetic sensibility is distinct from and beyond their own intellectual capacities.[3] Accustomed to their natural, fleshly knowledge securing for themselves a position of repute among the fleshly minded (38-39), *some* scholars[4] become unsettled when shown that their type of knowledge is not key to spiritual understanding. As the poet Eliot said: "Where is the wisdom we have lost in knowledge?"

HERODIANS AND PHARISEES (13-17)

> Whose is this image and superscription? And they said unto him, Caesar's. And Jesus answering said unto them, Render to Caesar the things that are Caesar's, and to God the things that are God's (17).

---

3. In his *Journal*, Fox tells of man who intended to set up a college to make ministers of Christ by making them scholars of "Hebrew, Greek, Latin, and the seven arts, which [Fox writes] were all but the teachings of the natural man, [and] not the way to make them ministers of Christ.... Then we showed him further, that Christ made his ministers himself, gave gifts unto them, and bid them 'Pray to the Lord of the harvest to send forth labourers'" (Fox, *Works*, 1:362-3).

4. Not every scholar is unsettled by the prophetic sensibility; some welcome the contribution, as is shown by the scribe who appears in verses 28 through 34.

In this brief interaction, Jesus brings into view the primary moral fault of both groups that approach him: the Herodians and the Pharisees. The Herodians were not a religious sect but a small political party that had joined forces with the larger, more powerful Pharisees.[5] Solely concerned with political power, they had thus rendered themselves in totality unto "Caesar," and thus had failed to render "to God the things that are God's."

The Pharisees here and elsewhere are shown to attend solely to the externalities of religion[6] (7:1–23); inwardly they are at variance with their outward demeanor and claims. In this passage, their hypocrisy is evident in their true but malevolent words (14) that cloak the intent "to catch [Jesus] in his words" (13). In keeping to their outward orientation, they ask Jesus about the act of giving tribute to Caesar: "Shall we give, or shall we not give?" (15) Jesus not only escapes the trap they lay for him[7] but also points to the Pharisees' failure to give tribute to God. For just as the penny is imprinted with Caesar's image, so is man created in the image of God: "So God created man in his own image, in the image of God created he him; male and female created he them" (Gen 1:27). And as the penny bearing Caesar's image belongs to Caesar, so man, created in the image of God, belongs to him. Jesus has moved the

---

5. "Whatever their [unknown] political aims, [the Herodians] early perceived that Christ's pure and spiritual teaching on the kingdom of God was irreconcilable with these, and that Christ's influence with the people was antagonistic to their interests" (Orr, *Encyclopaedia*, 3:1383).

6. "Jesus denounced the Pharisees more than He denounced any other class of the people. This seems strange when we remember that the main body of the religious people, those who looked for the Messiah, belonged to the Pharisees, and His teaching and theirs had a strong external resemblance. It was this external resemblance, united as it was with a profound spiritual difference, which made it incumbent on Jesus to mark Himself off from them. All righteousness with them was external, it lay in meats and drinks and divers washings.... He placed religion on a different footing, removed it into another region. With Him it was the heart that must be right with God, not merely the external actions; not only the outside of the cup and platter was to be cleansed, but the inside first of all" (Thompson, *Encyclopaedia*, 4:2365).

7. For Jesus to advise not to give tribute would put him at odds with the ruling political power, the Romans, while to advise giving tribute to Rome (Caesar) would alienate him from the people.

THE PRACTICE OF RELIGION (MARK 12)

Pharisees' attention from outward activity—paying or not paying tribute—to the inward, core obligation of man: to render himself unto God.

SADDUCEES (18-27)

The one defining mark of the Sadducees that is given in this passage is that they "say there is no resurrection" (18). According to the historian Josephus, they also denied divine Providence.[8] Because the Sadducees' understanding is stunted and their ignorance made insufferable by their smug, contemptuous manner, Jesus offers them nothing but a mirror to their mockery.[9]

THE SCRIBE (28-34)

In this passage, a thoughtful, earnest scribe asks Jesus, "Which is the first commandment of all?" (28) Up to this point, the chapter has featured one group of people after another, all claiming to revere and follow the Law yet all perverting the intent of the Law, which is to prepare its adherents to receive the kingdom of God. In contrast, this sole scribe, this individual, displays all the qualities necessary for entry into the kingdom: He has good discernment, "perceiv[ing] that he [Jesus] had answered them [the Sadducees] well" (28). He has an active desire to know, asking, "Which is the first commandment of all?" (28) He has a regard for truth, stating, "Well, Master, thou hast said the truth" (32). He is receptive, capable of learning, showing his grasp through his repetition of Jesus's teaching (32-33).

Chapter 12 has presented a hornets' nest of adversaries: the chief priests, the scribes, the elders, the Herodians, the Pharisees, and the Sadducees. After Jesus has defeated and dismissed them

---

8. "Their theology might be called 'religion within the limits of mere sensation'" (Thompson, *Encyclopaedia*, 4:2660), making the Sadducees the philosophical materialists of their day.

9. Closer examination of this passage can be found in the essay titled "Right Use of Our Tradition (12:18-34)."

all, however, there appears one, lone scribe who rises to the challenge of being, who faithfully responds to Truth; he, in his inward life, is thus prepared: "And when Jesus saw that he answered discreetly, he said unto him, Thou art not far from the kingdom of God" (34). This story of the single individual exemplifies the promise that the human being can rise in response to his calling, despite the surrounding wickedness or apathy to which humanity largely succumbs.

DAVID'S LORD OR SON

As if to quell any mistaken assumption that he supports the scribes as a group, Jesus directs his next two speeches against them (35, 38). In the first speech (35-37), Jesus shows his deep comprehension of the tradition's writings and contrasts that understanding with that of the scribes as a group, who can go no deeper than face-value literalism: the Messiah is to be "the son of David" (35), which to the scribes means that the Messiah is to be in the Davidic line. Jesus taunts them and their literalness by pointing out the contradiction: "David therefore himself calleth him Lord; and whence is he then his son?" (37)

The deeper, spiritual meaning of sonship is to have the essential nature of one who has come before. David and Jesus both manifested their kingship in Israel in that they each relied upon their Lord God; sat at his right hand, heard and carried out his commands; and thus saw their enemies defeated beneath their feet. It is this Lord that David, in large measure, consulted and that Jesus, without measure, embodied. That his flesh embodied the spirit of the Lord without measure qualifies Jesus as the Messiah and Lord.

This vignette has another function: it alludes to the many enemies Jesus has defeated earlier, as if to say, his sitting at the Lord's right hand—his attending to the Father's counsel—is the means by which he has vanquished the chief priests, scribes, elders, Pharisees, etc. Jesus has demonstrated and now teaches the people that in righteousness and reliance upon the Lord God, their strength

THE PRACTICE OF RELIGION (MARK 12)

to overcome worldly oppression is realized. "And the common people heard him gladly" (37).

THE PRACTICE OF RELIGION (38–44)

The final two teachings in this chapter consist of contrasting examples of the practice of religion: practice that is corrupt or superficial (38–41) as opposed to practice that is genuine and profound (42–44). Briefly summarized, the corruption in the scribes consists of relishing the perks that come with their privileged profession, using their power to take from the weak, and hiding their sin behind sanctimony. "These shall receive greater damnation" (38–40), Jesus avers. Superficial practice of religion entails proportioning some of one's worldly assets to its service (41), and perhaps in return enjoying an easy conscience and the esteemed aura of social respectability.

True expression of Christ-knowing religion arises in those who have realized that the world contains neither power nor riches to inwardly suffice (a condition symbolized by "the poor widow" [42]).[10] Suffering this truth, they willingly with gladness give over "even all [one's] living" (44). That is to say, we eagerly give over every resource of our personhood in love to God: "And thou shalt love the Lord thy God with all thy heart, and with all thy soul, and with all thy mind, and with all thy strength: this is the first commandment" (30).

> All Friends and brethren every where, walk in the truth, and know one another in the measure of life, that in it your minds may be guided up to the Father of life; and stand in his counsel, that he alone may be loved with all your strength, with all your minds, and with all your souls; so that ye may all know one another in the life and light, that ye may all be kept from idols. For if ye know

---

10. This same idea was expressed by George Fox: "[a]nd I saw all the world could do me no good. If I had had a king's diet, palace, and attendance, all would have been as nothing, for nothing gave me comfort but the Lord by his power" (*Works*, 1:75).

one another in the flesh only, that love which will rise out of that knowledge is feigned, and that will wither, and under the condemnation of the light must come.[11]

---

11. Fox, *Works*, 7:129.

Right Use of Our Tradition (12:18–34)

[A]nd many may have the Scriptures, and yet be very ignorant of, and strangers to, God's Holy Spirit; as the Jews were, who had them read in their synagogues every sabbath day, and yet Christ told them, "Ye neither know the Scriptures, nor the power of God."

—Isaac Penington

The words Penington quotes ("Ye neither know the Scriptures, nor the power of God") are from a passage in chapter 12 of Mark in which the Sadducees confront Jesus with their intent to deny the doctrine of resurrection. They, unlike the Pharisees, did not believe it possible to rise from the dead, and they make their case to Jesus by posing a comic scenario through which they subtly suggest the doctrine of resurrection is likewise ridiculous. Relying upon their knowledge and sophistry, the Sadducees appear to be satisfied with their way of using the tradition. In verses 19–23, they challenge Jesus:

> Master, Moses wrote unto us, If a man's brother die, and leave his wife behind him, and leave no children, that his brother should take his wife, and raise up seed unto his brother. Now there were seven brethren: and the first took a wife, and dying left no seed. And the second took her, and died, neither left he any seed: and the third

likewise. And the seven had her, and left no seed: last of all the woman died also. In the resurrection therefore, when they shall rise, whose wife shall she be of them? For the seven had her to wife.[1]

Jesus responds by diving deep below the surface of their silly question to reveal the error that had enabled them to ask it, namely, the words Penington quoted: "[They] neither know the Scriptures, nor the power of God." After identifying the underlying cause of their ignorance (and after delivering a short lesson on the status of those risen to new life [25]), Jesus proceeds to refute the Sadducees' "argument" against resurrection. His means of doing so mocks their self-assured but limited vision that Scripture's truth can be discovered by reason alone. And beyond that, Jesus seems to be having fun at the Sadducees' expense, for his manner of refuting their argument precisely mirrors their own attitude and technique in presenting it: Jesus likewise begins with a reference to Moses and then echoes the Sadducees' flamboyant confidence by implying his logic is so obvious and unassailable that he also needn't make the reasoning explicit. He says:

> And as touching the dead, that they rise: have ye not read in the book of Moses, how in the bush God spake unto him, saying, I am the God of Abraham, and the God of Isaac, and the God of Jacob? He is not the God of the dead but the God of the living: ye therefore do greatly err (26–27).

In his brief retort, Jesus uses two syllogisms to make his point. As both are implied, I've deconstructed them to reveal the logic of his argument:

SYLLOGISM #1

1st premise: If God is the God of Abraham, the God of Isaac, and the God of Jacob;

---

1. Epigraph. Penington, *Works*, 3:284. (The King James Version is cited here in verses 19–23 and is used throughout the essay.)

Right Use of Our Tradition (12:18-34)

2nd premise: And, if God is not the God of the dead, but the God of the living,

Conclusion: Then Abraham, Isaac, and Jacob are living.

Syllogism #2

1st premise: If Abraham, Isaac, and Jacob are living;

2nd premise: And if they have physically died,

Conclusion: Then there is resurrection from the dead.

Using logic, Jesus has adeptly, cleverly beaten the Sadducees at their own game. The Sadducees' method of interpretating Scripture is to strip words of spiritual meaning and then subject their lifeless husks to the overbearing rule of reason. The Sadducees would claim truth is served thereby, and that they—as literalistic logic-choppers—are the master purveyors of it.

Jesus does believe in resurrection but not as a result of the argument he's presented, which is as specious as the original question the Sadducees posed. Resurrection, as a concept, cannot be proved or denied using logic, emotion, study, sophistry, will, or presumption. Neither can it be understood before one has come into the knowledge of God (John 17:3); it is Christ inwardly known who is the resurrection and the life (John 11:25). C. S. Lewis shows the limits of intellect when he states:

> What we see in Satan is the horrible co-existence of a subtle and incessant intellectual activity with an incapacity to understand anything.[2]

Had the Sadducees asked a genuine question, they would have received a genuine answer, as does the scribe in the subsequent passage (28–34). The scribe has asked: "Which is the first commandment of all?" (28), and Jesus answers him:

> The first of all the commandments is Hear, O Israel; The Lord our God is one Lord: And thou shalt love the Lord thy God with all thy heart, and with all thy soul, and with

---

2. Jacobs, *1943*, 88.

all thy mind, and with all thy strength: this is the first commandment (29-30).

Jesus refers to the Law given by Moses (Deut 6:4-5), which calls the individual to rightly order his life, to gather his whole inward being (heart, soul, mind, strength) to one end: to love God. To prepare the individual to receive heaven's master, integrating principle of life is the Law's purpose, and Jesus echoes this intent by gathering the Law's many particulars into one commandment.

Right use of the Law is primarily to guide man toward integrated wholeness (perfection); the Sadducees recognize a different primary use for the Law: the promotion of social order. The Law becomes a means to order society through regulating social behavior and relations. Their nonsensical hypothesis of the seven brothers with one wife speaks to their need to define right relationships between and among people: "Whose wife shall she be?" they ask. That resurrection could pose an unresolvable absurdity in social relations is for them sufficient reason to discount it altogether as a doctrine of faith.

In addition to misapplying the Law, the Sadducees fragment it into minute particulars. For them, ethical life consists of fidelity to whatever precepts or duties are prescribed for particular situations. Their approach fragments moral life into something like a paint-by-number picture: when all the tiny, separate spaces have been filled with the prescribed color, there's an image, but it lacks creativity and life, just as the Sadducees observance of the Law— point by point—lacks the Life the Creator would have us know.

The Sadducees fragment the Law, and their hypothetical resurrection story trivializes it. Neither the fragmented nor the trivial is found in Jesus's answer to the scribe's question: "Which is the first commandment of all?" (28) Jesus repeats Deuteronomy 6:4-5 in all its dignified formality. In so answering the scribe's question with the original formal language given by Moses, Jesus affirms the tradition is to be revered; it stands as a repository of impermeable, sacred Truth. In his own words, the scribe recapitulates the statement he's heard. He thereby models the right approach to Scripture and tradition, as he is "duly applying them to [his]

Right Use of Our Tradition (12:18-34)

own state[s]" as George Fox wrote in his journal.[3] With the truth of Scripture resonating in his soul, the scribe can rely upon his own less formal speech to affirm what the tradition has held in keeping for him and for all. Having heard the scribe join with this commandment, Jesus can encourage him that he is "not far from the kingdom of God" (34).

There is one more point Jesus makes about the tradition and the need to have its precepts live within one's own being. This point is brought forward in verse 31:

> And the second [commandment] is like, namely this, Thou shalt love thy neighbour as thyself. There is none other commandment greater than these.

In adding this second commandment to the first given by Moses, Jesus provides an example of continuing revelation. When the Holy Spirit—that which has given us the tradition—is known, it will lead us whither it will into new understanding. Though new understanding can arise, it will be of a piece with the old, for both new and old arise from the same source, the same Holy Spirit of Truth. Says Jesus in preface to this new commandment: "And the second [commandment] is like" [unto the first] (31). Such continuity can only be revealed; it cannot be produced, for its mark is so delineated and refined as to be inimitable as life itself, for that is what it is.

These two stories in the book of Mark (the encounter with the Sadducees (18-27) and the exchange with the scribe (28-34) are back-to-back for this reason: they contrast right and wrong use of the Scriptures of our tradition. Wrong use is displayed by the Sadducees: spurious imposters who meddle with religion—employing worldly means and seeking worldly gain. Right use is evident in the scribe who shows the Scriptures' precepts to have become inherent to his being. The way Scriptures and the tradition are used—rightly or wrongly—is the end result of that which begins with character: that is, whether the drawings of Truth are heeded (John 6:44) or whether they are ignored and scorned. The

---

3. Fox, Nickalls, 31.

two stories show the result of each choice. Additionally, these stories contrast Jesus's evaluation and response to these different natures: taunting mockery to the Sadducees or earnest encouragement to the scribe.

It is the authentic, devoted seeker who speaks genuinely in simplicity of heart, who alone comes into the knowledge and kingdom of God. It is he who will be resurrected to new life; it is he who will come to affirm the tradition and sustain its vitality; and it is she who will come to read and understand the Scriptures "with profit and great delight."[4]

> For he that knows truth, that hath received from God the thing the Scriptures speak of, how easy is it to him to understand the words that speak of that thing! But he who hath the knowledge of the thing but from the words, how easy is it for him to misunderstand the words![5]

4. Fox, Nickalls, 32.
5. Penington, *Works*, 4:27.

You Shall Read Your Figures (Mark 13)

These are all figures; and as the sun without thee, so the sun of righteousness arising with healing in his wings within thee. All who mind the measure which God hath given you, it will open unto you these outward figures which God spake, and will teach you; as you go up and down you shall read your figures.

—GEORGE FOX[1]

THE TRACT FROM WHICH this epigraph was taken begins by telling the reader that it is "A Word from the Lord, to All the World and All Professors in the World; Spoken in Parables."[2] That is to say, Fox's message in this writing will be given largely in figurative language: in parables or figures of speech. Throughout this seven-page document, Fox repeatedly moves in and out of lists in which he compares the inward nature of man with outward things. Here is one example:

> As the night without thee and darkness, so there is night within; and as stars without thee, so there are stars within thee; as moon without thee, so there is moon within thee;

---

1. Fox, *Works*, 4:35.
2. Fox, *Works*, 4:32.

and as clouds without thee, so there are clouds within thee. These are all figures.[3]

"Figures," Fox writes elsewhere in this tract, "are spoken to the carnal part in man,"[4] that is to say, the unredeemed nature that has not yet known the appearance of Christ Within. Here in chapter 13 of Mark, Jesus—likewise using figurative language—informs four of his disciples of that which must befall them and every soul as it inwardly journeys from the unredeemed, carnal nature into the awareness of the "Lord of all . . . [who] is coming to fill his with the knowledge of himself."[5] As each soul progresses from the earthly, carnal state, it will come—figuratively speaking—to "see the Son of man coming in the clouds with great power and glory"[6] (13:26).

TWO OVERRIDING IDEAS (13:1-6)

In the opening passage of Mark 13, two overriding ideas preface the many allusions to the inward journey that comprise the bulk of the chapter. The first idea is presented in the opening exchange as Jesus and his disciples exit the temple; one of the disciples, marveling at the new buildings, says, "Master, see what manner of stones and what buildings *are here!*" (1). The new temple buildings were man-made structures whose purpose was to house the society's religious and legal practices. In this exchange, however, they stand as figures for man-made religion: communal ideas of the nature of God, faith, salvation, sacrifice, prayer, virtue, ethics, laws, hierarchy, custom, and practice: in sum, everything: every idea about religion that has been formed or housed in the mind, soul, and heart of the people. All of it, says Jesus, must go: every idea comprising the religious bulwark is to be so thoroughly stripped of meaning and allegiance that "there shall not be left one stone upon another" (2). The outward or fleshly system of belief by which one

3. Fox, *Works*, 4:34.
4. Fox, *Works*, 4:34.
5. Fox, *Works*, 4:34.
6. The King James Version of the Bible is used throughout the essay.

YOU SHALL READ YOUR FIGURES (MARK 13)

had hitherto structured one's life must tumble down in this time of personal apocalypse, of moving from man-made religion (or from a philosophy) to revealed faith.

The second idea that opens this chapter anticipates the natural but faulty response to this bewildering loss of spiritual bearings. Jesus warns those who find themselves in this empty, precarious position to resist any replacement ideology that is touted by others. "Take heed lest any man deceive you: For many shall come in my name, saying, I am Christ; and shall deceive many" (5-6). Accepting that one has no solid footing during this time is as essential as it is distressing, and one must reject and ignore any whose eagerness to exalt themselves drives them to seek the adulation of others, as well as reject the urge to integrate oneself into communities that offer ready-made identity to the estranged self.

THE BEGINNINGS OF SORROWS (7-9)

Having set out the overriding ideas that the soul's desolation is a sign that inward transformation is at hand and that one must guard against false prophets and conformity at this precarious time, Jesus turns to figurative language to convey the magnitude of disturbance that is to be expected. In severity, the inward trauma will be akin to the effects of war, multiple earthquakes, and famine, and "these are [only] the beginnings" (7-8).

A TESTIMONY AGAINST THEM (9-11)

There is a widespread notion that in the apocalyptic discourse found in each of the three synoptic gospels[7] Jesus speaks literally, foretelling an outward event: that the catastrophe he describes will occur at a single point in time and will be experienced simultaneously throughout the world. In verse 9, that notion is dispelled as Jesus tells his disciples that during this great tribulation they

---

7. The three synoptic gospels each have an apocalyptic chapter: chapter 24 in Matthew, chapter 13 in Mark, and chapter 21:5-36 in Luke.

should expect persecution from "rulers and kings" and in "councils and in the synagogues." Obviously, were this time he speaks of to be a single, global event, these authorities would likewise be affected, whereas they are not and instead retain the avidity to persecute those who minister the gospel. Anticipating the persecution his disciples will face, Jesus rehearses the mission, method, and credentials that they, as apostles, must take on:

> [A]nd ye shall be brought before rulers and kings for my sake, for a testimony against them. And the gospel must first be published among all nations. But when they shall lead you and deliver you up, take no thought beforehand what ye shall speak, neither do ye premeditate: but whatsoever shall be given you in that hour, that speak ye: for it is not ye that speak, but the Holy Ghost (9b–11).

THE SOUL'S AFFLICTION (12–14)

Jesus then begins to funnel the outward, grand-scale catastrophes (figuratively described as war, earthquakes, and famine) into their true and actual location: the individual soul. The great devastation will be experienced inwardly—within each individual and at a particular time. This is indicated by the type of figurative language Jesus begins to use: it is personal. Example after example is given of the most personal and extreme devastation: betrayal and murder within the family. "Now the brother shall betray the brother to death, and the father the son; and children shall rise up against their parents, and shall cause them to be put to death" (12).

Listing affliction upon affliction, Jesus goes on: "And ye shall be hated of all men for my name's sake" (13a). He here expresses the utter isolation and alienation one must undergo in fidelity to—at this low point of emptiness and confusion—one knows not what. Only in hindsight can one piece together words to describe the experience of "enduring unto the end" (13b) as a lonely fidelity to the heart or core of one's being in its inviolable purity and life; perhaps it could be called fidelity to the nameless, intrinsic holy covenant. The harrowing experience of dying to the self is regularly recorded in seventeenth-century Friends' journals, and Fox, in his *Journal*, describes it in this way:

> When I was in the deep, under all shut up, I could not believe that I should ever overcome; my troubles, my sorrows, and my temptations were so great, that I often thought I should have despaired, I was so tempted.[8]

In verse 14, Jesus returns to the prophet Daniel's words to describe this universal, desolate, and pivotal condition as seeing "the abomination of desolation."[9]

LEAVING THE WORLDLY SELF (14b-23)

In this passage, Jesus uses figurative language to convey the idea that the old, worldly way must be totally left behind. In verses 14b through 18, he uses the figure of a refugee, abandoning his or her home for a better, higher place: "flee to the mountains" (14); "on the housetop [don't] go down into the house" (15). All that one clings to as one's own, all that has defined and distinguished one, no longer applies: the covering garment of the constructed self can no longer be taken up (16). Leaving the old worldly self, dying to that self, will occur at the farthest edge of our capacity to endure, and we should pray that no additional difficulty be added during this transition; carrying or nursing a child (17) or traveling in winter (18) are figures that convey added difficulty.

For each person, the severity of the plight is an unparalleled "affliction, such as was not from the beginning of the creation which God created unto this time, neither shall be" (19). For in this void, this formless darkness of the soul, the spirit of God is moving

---

8. Fox, *Works*, 1:74.

9. "When Daniel undertook to specify an abomination so surpassingly disgusting to the sense of morality and decency, and so aggressive against every thing that was godly as to drive all from its presence and leave its abode desolate, he chose this as the strongest among several synonyms, adding the qualification 'that maketh desolate.' (Dan 11:31; 12:11)." (Hirsch, *Encyclopaedia*, 1:16).

upon face of the waters. His is the wisdom; his is the judgment to measure out the time the flesh can endure before salvation is given: that is to say, before the elect Seed, Christ Within, is known (20). As he wills, will he pronounce: "Let there be light" (Gen 1:3), and with that pronouncement, Christ, "the beginning of the creation of God" (Rev 3:14), is revealed within: the Inward Christ is now seen and known.

Jesus warns once again: at the height of one's tribulation, one may be tempted to attach oneself to a teacher whose doctrine appears sound or whose manner is charismatic ("Lo, here is Christ; or lo, he is there" [21]). There will be such a longing for relief from this greatest of troubles, this unsought nihilism, that temptation to settle "for false Christs and false prophets" will be strong. We have been warned (23).

COMING TO THE END (24-25)

> But in those days, after that tribulation, the sun shall be darkened, and the moon shall not give her light, And the stars of heaven shall fall, and the powers that are in heaven shall be shaken (24-25).

The imagery in these two verses is of light found in nature—the sun, moon, and stars. We are being told in a figurative way that the nature previously relied upon, our human nature, is no longer adequate: no longer is our nature capable of lighting our way, as the sun does in the day and the moon at night. The lights of nature are now darkened and giving no light. What we had previously looked up to guide our way through the dark night (as historically, man has looked to the stars) has now fallen; the values we had exalted, that we had deemed "heavenly," are shaken and no longer seen as reliable. Through having endured the long suffering of dying to the self, dying to the first birth, the person comes to a standstill: the worldly, carnal life has been downed and darkened, and one is without hope.

YOU SHALL READ YOUR FIGURES (MARK 13)

THE BEGINNING OF THE CREATION OF GOD (26-27)

> And then shall they see the Son of man coming in the clouds with great power and glory. And then shall he send his angels, and shall gather together his elect from the four winds, from the uttermost part of the earth to the uttermost part of heaven (26-27).

The Son of man comes from beyond: not by earthly means and not from the earthly realm, for the Son of man is not of the earth. He is transcendent and bears the image of God, for he is the Son of God and is become the Son of man: the one who comes after the first man, the first birth, the first Adam. The elect Seed will gather all together who have known this miraculous second birth, this second Adam, as they will recognize him when he is manifested in the writings and speech of others, though they be far distant from one another in worldly, fleshly similitude: different in race, gender, language, age, nationality, time, and place; the elect Seed shall be gathered by his messengers (27): that which informs the mind with Truth.

JESUS PROVIDES CONTEXT (28-31)

Early in this chapter, the disciples had asked for a sign that would indicate the approaching fulfillment or completion of all things (4). Jesus has answered their request in this long discourse, which he then caps with a short parable about a fig tree leafing out as a sign summer is near (28). This brief parable is a reminder that all he has said "in like manner" (29) has been spoken in figures.

The words "this generation shall not pass, till all these things be done" (30) has been used to support the interpretation that throughout this discourse Jesus has been predicting an event in time: the destruction of the temple in Jerusalem that will occur in 70 AD. That is to say, the word "generation" is interpreted to mean those present whose life spans will enable them to witness the temporal event of the temple's destruction. Continuing the thought begun in verse 30, however, the following verse 31, ("Heaven and earth shall pass away; but my words shall not pass away") places Jesus's words in these two verses within a timeless context, not the temporal one that has been touted by literalists. Jesus speaks of God's redemptive activity within the generation (the Greek word is *genea*[10]) of the first Adam, and his will for fallen humankind's redemption continues constant "till all these things be done": that is, until each and all are of the *genea* of the second Adam, as told us by "the faithful and true witness" (Rev 3:14) whose "words shall not pass away" (31).

I SAY UNTO ALL (32-37).

The final passage in this chapter contains a parable that not only underscores the figurative use of language throughout the discourse but also tells of our worldly predicament. Only God the Father can redeem/perfect us by sending his Son into our hearts

---

10. In a *Wikipedia* article titled "Olivet Discourse," two scholars (Iver Larsen and Philip La Grange du Toit) support the idea that the word "generation" in verse 30 is used to mean a "kind of people"; they agree that the word does not refer to those whose life spans coincide in time. Though the two scholars agree the Greek word *genea* (in the KJV translated as "generation") means a "kind of people," they disagree on whether Jesus refers to "the 'good' kind of people . . . who . . . will endure through all the tribulations" (Larsen) or "the 'bad' kind of people" (La Grange du Toit) based on Jesus's use of the word in Matthew 23:33. In my essay, I specify that the "kind of people" to which Jesus refers when he uses the word "generation" in verse 30 are the unredeemed: those living in the first birth, the first Adam "kind of people." Jesus is saying each human being (that is, all humankind) will remain in his present unredeemed state—not knowing Christ, the Light Within—until he or she has undergone the dying to the self that Jesus has laid out figuratively in this discourse. (I would paraphrase verses 30 and 31 in this prosaic way: I tell you the kind of people who are in the unredeemed condition will remain unredeemed until they've gone through this great tribulation that I've told you about. This fact will not change but will be forever true for all humankind.) In verses 30-31, Jesus is emphasizing the necessity of undergoing the inward cross: that there is no other way for a human being (humankind) to come to know resurrection in Christ (the second birth), and never will there be another way: his "words shall not pass away" (31).

You Shall Read Your Figures (Mark 13)

that we too may become, as daughters and sons of God, his own creation, bearing his image. Until then, Jesus names us "servants" (34) who are to await the arrival of "the master of the house (35), the "house" being a figure for our fleshly habitation. We have "every man his work"—courageous fidelity to truth in the heart—and must watch for our master, the Son of man (34), to arrive. That this instruction is not solely addressed to Jesus's disciples but applies universally to everyone is the final idea in this powerful discourse on the inward progress of each soul as it journeys through the great tribulation and into the great joy: "And what I say unto you I say unto all, Watch" (37).

> Beloved, think it not strange concerning the fiery trial which is to try you, as though some strange thing happened unto you: But rejoice, inasmuch as ye are partakers of Christ's sufferings; that, when his glory shall be revealed, ye may be glad also with exceeding joy (1 Pet 4:12–13).

The Way Shown (Mark 14)

It is conceived in sorrow, and brought forth without any to pity it; nor does it murmur at grief and oppression. It never rejoices but through sufferings, for with the world's joy it is murdered. I found it alone, being forsaken.

—JAMES NAYLER

IN CHAPTER 13 OF Mark's Gospel, Jesus used figurative language to describe the suffering each and every soul must endure prior to receiving the Light of Christ Within. In chapter 14, we see Jesus enter into his own particular tribulation, and thus we are provided with the archetype for each of our own journeys through the world. In chapter 13, we were told the way forward; in chapter 14, we are being shown that way.

Though the circumstances of Jesus's tribulation will be uniquely his own, the particulars point to the universal formation that every person must undergo, each in his own distinct time and place, each with her own unique history and circumstances. Chapter 14 presents a template of the conflict; error; corruption, both personal and institutional; violence; cruelty; pain; shame; abandonment; and isolation that one suffers in a life that is lived over the decades. For Jesus, however, all the injury happens within a few days. Regardless of the intensity of his ordeal, he steadily assures us—and perhaps himself—throughout the account that

THE WAY SHOWN (MARK 14)

this apparent calamity is in accord with God's will; it is all to be expected, for this is the one and only true way to eternal life.

TROUBLE WITHOUT AND WITHIN (1-11)

In this chapter, there are two groups of characters that bring about Jesus's suffering and death: the corrupt religious establishment and the uncomprehending disciples. Judas's betrayal is the act which brings the two groups' determinants—corruption and ignorance—together and amalgamates them into a force capable of inflicting the suffering Jesus will endure. The opening passage of the chapter, verses 1 through 11, introduces all three of these components: (1) the corruption of the religious establishment, (2) the ignorance of the disciples, and (3) the betrayal of Judas.

The chief priests' and scribes' treachery is exposed immediately in the first two verses of the chapter: "After two days was the feast of the passover, and of unleavened bread: and the chief priests and the scribes sought how they might take him by craft, and put him to death" (1).[1] While Israel makes plans to celebrate its historic deliverance from captivity and oppression (the exodus from Egypt), its chief priests plot to destroy the one who would have all know deliverance from inward captivity and oppression. These religious leaders should be celebrating and advancing the people's freedom, but instead they plot their continued captivity, and thus the institution is corrupted.

Next in this introductory passage is a short story (3-9) that reveals the disciples' failure to understand Jesus. In "the anointing at Bethany," the disciples criticize a woman who has honored Jesus by anointing him with costly oil; the disciples see the act as wasteful and would have had the money used to serve the poor. Jesus justifies the woman's having "done what lay in her power" (8), thereby siding with one who acts with personal initiative, understanding, and love for him. The disciples argue that virtue is the function of principle and outward, social action while Jesus

---

1. Epigraph. Nayler, *Works*, 4:382. The King James Version is used throughout the essay.

teaches virtue is an expression of the heart. Furthermore, Jesus sides with a woman who is jointly criticized by a group of men. His claim that the whole world will honor her act wherever the gospel is proclaimed (9) reverses the power imbalance begun with the disciples' joint castigation. The disciples find power in the crowd; Jesus finds power in righteousness.[2]

Finally, completing the introductory passage, are two verses that bring together the corruption of the religious leaders and the ignorance of the disciples: Judas Iscariot is "one of the twelve [and he] went unto the chief priests, to betray [Jesus] unto them" (10). The priests' and Judas's complicity is registered in the next verse, and their joint force is now complete and active: "And he sought how he might conveniently betray him" (11).

JUST AS HE HAD TOLD THEM (12–31)

Given that the destructive force is now in place and set to act, it is imperative to show that Jesus is aware of all that has passed, is passing, and will come to pass. The narrator must show that Jesus has a higher, truer grasp of reality, beyond mere human capacity. To the human and limited understanding, Jesus will be broken and killed; however, on the true, divine platform of reality, Jesus is supreme; unconquered; and wholly, fully in control.[3] These expansive, divine qualities are shown *figuratively* in his ability to foresee the future.

In the first five verses of this section (12–16), the narrator depicts Jesus as having a more-than-human foresight of the complex sequence of events that will allow him and his disciples to conveniently organize and enjoy the Passover supper. The implication is

---

2. The prophecy in this passage of the gospel's spread throughout the world through preaching (9) not only underscores the disciples' future responsibility but also tells of the ultimate triumph of the gospel, the power of God. The accuracy of Jesus's prophecies in this chapter shows him to be knowledgeable and in control, though by the end of the chapter, all will appear to be in disarray.

3. Unity with God—wherever that leads—is synonymous with victory. Where one stands in the worldly hierarchy is ultimately inconsequential.

THE WAY SHOWN (MARK 14)

that if Jesus has such detailed prescience of this minor accommodation, he certainly is able to foresee events of major importance. And during the Passover meal, this implication is borne out when he alerts his disciples that one of them will betray him (18), that he [Jesus] will die (25), that all of the disciples will fail him (27), that he will be resurrected and lead the way into Galilee (28), and that the cock will crow twice and Peter deny him thrice (30).

Not only does Jesus's envisioning the future designate him as having divine power, but when all that he has forecasted has come to pass, his disciples (and we readers) must conclude that this trial of suffering and death is, in fact, the will of God. That Jesus twice refers to Scriptures as having foretold the course set out for the Son of man (21, 27) again confirms that an amendatory tribulation is in fact God's will throughout time.[4]

ACCEPTANCE (32-52)

Hitherto in the stories of Mark's Gospel, Jesus has led and taught his disciples, and he has shown all his opponents to be no match for him in virtue and power. We have seen Jesus in this role of the god-like man and have rightly attributed his greater-than-human ability to his knowledge of; reliance upon; and unity with God, the Father. In this passage, however, that knowledge of, reliance upon, and unity with "Abba, Father" (36) requires him to forfeit all the preeminence that has been given him in the world, and thus outward manifestations of his commanding strength are largely absent. He is unable to summon his three closest disciples to stay alert while he prays, and he is betrayed by another who's in league with his long-standing, corrupt opponents. Arrested upon their orders, Jesus is treated as a lowly thief (48).

In this passage, strength of spirit is not exhibited outwardly by directing or defeating others; rather the fleshly will is directed inward to subdue or discipline itself that God may rule. Jesus

---

4. The suffering and death is scandalous to the person who refuses the God of Truth; God does not align with any imposed fantasy of what constitutes divine love.

yields: "nevertheless not what I will, but what thou wilt" (36). The movement from following his own will to accepting the Father's is replicated in his response to both groups: the disciples and the religious leaders (through the proxy of the armed crowd sent to arrest him).

Jesus instructs his disciples to stay awake while he struggles and prays: once and again, praying the same words (39) with utmost determination. A third time he returns to the disciples after praying, and this time he accepts their failure and says, "Sleep on now, and take your rest: it is enough" (41). Similarly, with the posse sent by the religious leaders, Jesus at first challenges them, but then reverses himself and tolerates their duplicity, stating it's been preordained in the Scriptures: "I was daily with you in the temple teaching, and ye took me not; but the scriptures must be fulfilled" (49). Once Jesus has inwardly accepted the Father's will, he is able to "endure unto the end" (13:13b) the weakness, failure, and corrupt abuse of the world.

CONCLUSION (53-72)

The final passage in chapter 14 takes place within the stronghold of corruption: the high priest's palace where all the religious leaders—the priests, elders, and scribes—are assembled, with the intent to find an excuse to put Jesus to death. In this passage, which comprises more than a quarter of this long chapter's length, Jesus speaks little. He knows what is to happen, has accepted and will not oppose it, for it is God's will. Only once does he speak, and with words that will enrage the religious leaders and give them the "evidence" they seek to condemn him of blasphemy. Jesus answers the high priest's question "Art thou the Christ, the Son of the most Blessed?" (61) with these words: "I am: and ye shall see the Son of man sitting on the right hand of power, and coming in the clouds of heaven" (62).[5]

---

5. It is interesting to note that Jesus's claim would not be a threat to the innocent; for speaking to his disciples previously, he used some of the same words to describe salvation: "And then shall they see the Son of man coming in

The Way Shown (Mark 14)

We have seen the corrupt force of the leaders gather momentum throughout chapter 14: first the plotting of Jesus's death, then colluding with Judas, followed by the false arrest and condemning Jesus "to be guilty of death" (64). Finally, these corrupted ones abuse the dignity and person of Jesus (65). Only killing him remains to be done in this most extreme portrayal of human suffering at the hand of the corrupt.

As the religious leaders have done their worst, so likewise must the other group, the disciples, be shown to fail Jesus in the most extreme way. Through a kiss (45), a gesture of love, one disciple has betrayed Jesus, and during the arrest, "all [his disciples] forsook him, and fled" (50). Peter, the most ardently outspoken of the Twelve, follows Jesus to the high priest's palace, and while Jesus is tried within by the kangaroo court, Peter warms his flesh by a courtyard fire. Accused by a serving girl, Peter's three-time cowardly denial is in high contrast to his earlier claims of loyalty (29, 31). His shamed weeping ends the story, a fitting conclusion to the chapter in which Jesus has entered knowingly into his great tribulation, subject to all the failure, corruption, cruelty, pain, shame, abandonment, and desolation that the world can muster against a living soul.

---

the clouds with great power and glory" (13:26). To these corrupt leaders, however, these words cannot be heard but as a threat of their damnation. That the same words (voice) can effect different responses—depending upon the soul's guilt or innocence—is the meaning of these verses: "Marvel not at this: for the hour is coming, in the which all that are in the graves shall hear his voice, And shall come forth; they that have done good, unto the resurrection of life; and they that have done evil, unto the resurrection of damnation" (John 5:28–29).

Seeing It Through (Mark 15)

THIS PAST MONTH MY daughter sent me a podcast in which was recounted the life history of Benjamin Lay, an early abolitionist and Quaker of the eighteenth century. Lay often acted as would a modern performance artist, engaging in inventive acts for a political cause: he sought to shame slaveholding Quakers into an awareness of their cruelty and hypocrisy. Unsurprisingly, his performances were not well-received, and in 1738, he was disowned by Abington (Pa.) Meeting. Lay retreated from Quaker society to live in a cave not far from the meetinghouse, his abode furnished with a private library of two hundred books. Centuries have passed, and Lay, once deemed a gadfly, is now hailed a hero.

How does the sequence of Lay's critique of and then retreat from society pertain to chapter 15 of the Gospel of Mark? In both instances, the Light of the Word exposed the dark spirit, which, in turn, strove to overcome it by silencing the speaker through banishment or death. With the darkness exposed and his work done, the prophet in each case became silent, leaving the corrupted social body to itself: either to acknowledge the reality the Light had revealed, or to refuse to see and to remain in darkness.[1]

In the several decades following the testimony of Benjamin Lay, the Society of Friends slowly moved toward accepting the reality that slaveholding is sin, and in 1776—seventeen years after

---

1. "Here lies the test: the light has come into the world, but men preferred darkness to light because their deeds were evil" (John 3:19). I've relied primarily on the New English Bible throughout this essay. When I've used the King James Version, I've so indicated in the text.

Seeing It Through (Mark 15)

Lay's death—Philadelphia Yearly Meeting (a regional organization of Friends) deemed the owning of slaves to be an offense requiring disownment.

In Mark 15, which tells of Jesus's crucifixion and death, we find the same pattern that regularly occurs when Light has shone forth in darkness: there follows worldly persecution; prophetic silence; and ultimately, the world's acknowledgment of truth. In this narrative, however, the sequence is greatly compressed in time: the apprehension of truth comes moments after Jesus's death. First to speak, a centurion, seeing "how [Jesus] died . . . said, 'Truly this man was a son of God'" (39). That this expression of convincement was uttered by one so greatly averse to the Way (being a supporter of empire as well as an executioner) portends the universal restoration of humanity to its true state of seeing and becoming sons of God.

CONTAGION (1-32)

Before reaching the centurion's words, however, the chapter reviews the labyrinth of iniquity through which Jesus, silent and unresisting, is dragged. The first two-thirds of chapter 15 illustrate the spread of corruption and ignorance—up, down, and throughout the social hierarchy. Pilate, a Roman prefect (governor), wields imperial power and therefore is in society's highest echelon; he is petitioned by the chief priests to treat Jesus as a criminal (1–3). At the other end of the social spectrum are the people, whom the priests stir up to cry out for Jesus's crucifixion (11, 13–14). So tainted is the society with the dark, demonic spirit that nowhere can be found the pure Light of Truth, and Jesus is all but silent, knowing that this is the way of things.

His one statement throughout his captivity is in response to Pilate's question: "Are you the king of the Jews?" Jesus doesn't answer him directly yes or no (thereby denying the prefect's power) but instead makes Pilate himself an unwitting exponent of truth when he answers: "The words are yours" (2).

Jesus's refusal to speak in his own defense during the remainder of his ordeal implies his early statement to Pilate stands applicable to every opposition he encounters. His continuous silence drives home the fact that the violators' words and actions are their own—their responsibility alone—and not his. He will not take part in, cooperate, nor assert himself (5); neither does he engage them nor accept their tender mercies (23), for to do so would give latitude to yet more self-deception in their already corrupted souls. If Jesus were to take part in the proceedings—even to resist—his participation would allow the persecutors to claim that he had brought upon himself the treatment he receives, and as such, that he should bear the burden for what is, in fact, their sin. Even Pilate can see that the responsibility for this travesty lies upon the chief priests and their malice (10).

This glimmer of insight shown by Pilate does not absolve him of corruption, only of ignorance. His interaction with the mob regarding Barabbas, the prisoner to be released (6–15), recalls the populist politician who can "whip up the crowd into a mob frenzy."[2] In his first receiving Jesus from the chief priests and then delivering him to the soldiers to be flogged and crucified (15), Pilate is the center link in the chain of crime. It is this "division of labor" that allows each party to deceive themselves into thinking they are absolved of responsibility for wrongdoing; thus Jesus's arrest, trial, persecution, and death illustrates the most spiritually dangerous, destructive configuration of "the prince of this world": collusion among the wicked.

DARKNESS OVER THE WHOLE LAND (33-37)

That Jesus is the "king of the Jews" is a motif woven throughout chapter 15. Early in the chapter in verse 2, Pilate asks Jesus directly: "Are you the king of the Jews?" Later before the crowd, Pilate uses the phrase to rile the mob (9, 12). For the soldiers, it provides opportunity to address Jesus mockingly (18), and as a criminal charge, it is inscribed above Jesus's body on the cross (26). Finally,

2. Raskin, *Unthinkable*.

Seeing It Through (Mark 15)

in a vile culmination of corruption and ignorance, the chief priests and scribes use the term "king of Israel" to mock Jesus as he dies:

> Let the Messiah, the king of Israel, come down now from the cross. If we see that, we shall believe (32).[3]

This chapter has steadily, increasingly brought the darkness of moral and intellectual error to the fore. That is to say, corruption and ignorance have become acute. So severe does the darkness become that it envelopes the land, though the sun be at its zenith in "the sixth hour" (33). Lasting three hours (three, in Hebrew, being the number of completeness) "until the ninth hour," we are being told that the darkness is at its greatest intensity. At this point, Jesus's words come forth: "*Eli, Eli, lema sabachthani?*" (34) Sensing abandonment, being forsaken by God, is to have lost sight and hope: the darkness is absolute.

That Jesus speaks these despairing words in Aramaic, his native tongue, rather than the Hebrew in which Psalm 22 (from which these words come) was written is interpreted in this way: individual, personal experience of the typology of Scripture is required of everyone. The cross is personal and inward, as early Friends knew and preached.[4]

Though the corruption of the priests is no longer on view at this point in the narrative, the darkness of ignorance remains, and verse 36 gives us the chapter's final expression of spiritual blindness

---

3. The priests' insistence upon Jesus meeting their skewed criterion of Messiahship is tantamount to their claiming themselves to be the arbiters of good and evil, that is, to "be as gods, knowing good and evil" (Gen 3:5). This lie is the serpent's temptation that led to humanity's fall from grace. It is appropriate that this particular offense (which is echoed in the same verse by the thieves' taunting) appears in the narrative at the point of greatest darkness, for it was the first sin in Eden and is shown to be the last at Golgotha: suggesting that—first and last—to exalt the limited, natural perspective is the root of all sin, the sin of pride. That the error issues from both the priests and the thieves tells us that whether high-up or low-down, all are guilty who presume to judge—to discern good from evil—while constrained by the fallen nature of the first Adam.

4. That the cross must be borne by everyone is suggested by the figure of Simon the Cyrenian, an everyman passerby, who was required to carry the cross (21).

as portrayed by the bystanders who mistake Jesus's words for a call to Elijah: "Hark, he is calling Elijah. . . . Let us see . . . if Elijah will come to take him down" (35-36). With Jesus's death (37), even the darkness of ignorance is overcome: following the rending of the temple veil that figuratively separated God and man, the centurion states: "Truly this man was a son of God" (39).

OUTSPREADING (40-47)

First evidenced in the centurion, awareness of and right regard for Jesus grows steadily throughout the remainder of this chapter and into the next. The growth is first seen in numbers, as women—many women—who followed, ministered, or came with Jesus to Jerusalem look on, though they be far off, and thus their vision is but small. Yet watchful from a distance, the women see the Son of man, the master of the house (13:33-37).

Right regard for Jesus gains ground within the social hierarchy when next appears one who is individuated by name: Joseph of Arimathaea. As an individual and a male, Joseph not only stands in patriarchally favored contrast to the group of women, but more significantly, as an individual who is named, Joseph stands apart from the undifferentiated cackle of corrupt priests. The contrast between them and Joseph is further heightened by the fact that though the priests and Joseph are peers in the Council (the Sanhedrin, which was the supreme court of the Jews), only Joseph is described as "a respected member of the Council" (43).

As a "respected" member of the highest court, Joseph is distinguished as having good judgment. In the same verse, we learn that he "waited for the kingdom of God" (43 [KJV]). That these two facts occur in the same verse suggests there is a correlation between good judgment and waiting to receive God's kingdom (as is done in Friends' meeting for worship).

Joseph understands that God and his kingdom must be waited for: that he himself is not a god, and therefore he does not exalt himself by claiming that he need not wait but perpetually inhabits the kingdom. In contrast, the priests (neither differentiated

Seeing It Through (Mark 15)

nor esteemed) see themselves "as gods knowing good and evil," thus claiming for themselves a power of judgement that they do not have. The text implies that one must wait for and receive the virtue and power of God to judge righteously: to be enabled to distinguish good from evil, King from subject, and Christ from self. One must know the difference experientially before one can make a distinction intellectually (1 Cor 6:2 [KJV]).

Joseph makes this distinction, and therefore he waits for the kingdom of God, thereby showing the good judgment for which he is respected. To reinforce the idea that Joseph's waiting is the preparation needed to receive the kingdom, he appears on "Preparation-day (that is, the day before the Sabbath)" (42), which suggests that Joseph judiciously prepares for the Rest to come: he prepares and waits for the kingdom of God (43).

Second, we see that Joseph is not only a man of humility and good judgment but also a man of courage and one who takes responsibility: Joseph "bravely went in to Pilate and asked for the body of Jesus" (43); he, at his own cost, then provides Jesus with a respectful burial (46). Joseph's actions mirror in reverse those of the priests who delivered Jesus to Pilate (1) and treated him disrespectfully (32).

In verse 44, we see Pilate continue his policy of questioning others (2, 4, 9, 12, and 14) and letting their answers determine his actions: he thus equips himself at every turn with the opportunity to deny personal responsibility. (And therein is he contrasted with Joseph.) In this passage, after questioning the centurion (44), Pilate—ever the middleman—releases the body to Joseph: the death effected as much by his lack of moral responsibility as by the priests' and people's villainy.

In the next and final chapter of the Gospel of Mark, we will see a continuation and acceleration of the forward momentum toward regard for and knowledge of Jesus as Lord. In chapter 15, however, the story ends with the women standing by: women who are named, individuated; waiting; alert; and watchful.

> And Mary Magdala and Mary the mother of Joseph were watching and saw where he was laid (47).

Taking In and Giving Out (Mark 16)

When we read the parables of the Good Samaritan or the Prodigal Son, our first question is not, did this really happen? Rather we ask, is this true? Or even better, we ask, in what way is this true for me? Does this correspond to my own experience? [George] Fox seemed to read not just the parables but the entire Bible as a parable, constantly asking how it applied to his own condition.

—Tom Gates

NO CONSIDERATION OF MARK'S Gospel is complete without an attempt to explain the seeming rupture between the first and second halves of its last chapter. The first eight verses of the chapter follow the women to the tomb, and from there, we see them leave: amazed and afraid. Though instructed to "tell his [Jesus's] disciples and Peter"[1] that he will show himself to them in Galilee (7), the women said nothing to anyone (8). The second half of the chapter then begins afresh with a completely different narrative. Jesus is present, active, and appearing to Mary Magdalene: the same Mary who visited the tomb with two other women in the first half of the chapter, in which none of them saw or received instruction from

---

1. Epigraph. Gates, *Friends Journal*. The King James Version is used here and throughout the essay.

Taking In and Giving Out (Mark 16)

Jesus. The explicit ending of the first half in which the women are silent about their experience is contradicted in the second half, where Mary Magdalene "went and told [the disciples] that [she] had been with [Jesus] . . . that he was alive, and had been seen of her" (10–11).

This disjointed post-crucifixion narrative can be most usefully examined, I believe, in the way that George Fox and other early Friends would have examined it: the way described by Friend Tom Gates in the epigraph. A careful look at the text brings to mind the inward experience that reconciles the discordant halves into coherent spiritual knowledge and teaching. One realizes the writer's intent could not have been better accomplished by a conventional realistic narrative, and one finishes the reading amazed and full of gratitude.

PART ONE (1–8)

The first two verses of part one set forth its theme: the old is past, and the new has begun. The first verse tells of custom and tradition, the old guides of the past: "And when the sabbath was past, Mary Magdalene, and Mary the mother of James, and Salome, had bought sweet spices, that they might come and anoint him." Tradition directs and orders the attending women's thoughts and actions: they've waited until "the sabbath was past," for in the tradition, all are commanded "to keep the sabbath";[2] they've bought spices to anoint the body, for it is the custom to honor and care for the dead.[3]

In contrast with the first verse's focus on the old, verse 2 refers solely to the new: "And very early in the morning the first day of the week, they came unto the sepulchre at the rising of the sun." It is a new day ("very early in the morning"); it is a new week ("the first day of the week"). They arrive at the tomb "at the rising of the sun" (2).

---

2. ". . . therefore the Lord thy God commanded thee to keep the sabbath day" (Deut 5:15b).

3. *K'vod-hameit* is a term meaning "[l]iterally, 'respect/honor for the dead.' In Jewish tradition, preparing a body and holding a prompt funeral are important ways to honor the deceased," as stated by Union for Reform Judaism.

Carrying the theme of old and new into the next two verses, we learn that the women have come with their customary expectations and reasoning: a great stone will be blocking the entry to the tomb; they haven't enough strength to move it themselves; they'll need to find help from others (3). Expectation and reasoning block their way, like a great stone; they operate by the old human way of assessing, calculating, and petitioning. In the new way of things, however, their old nature with its reliance on tradition, reason, and assumption is transcended: the stone is removed, and the entranceway is clear.

THE YOUNG MAN

> And they all forsook him, and fled. And there followed him a certain young man, having a linen cloth cast about his naked body; and the young men laid hold on him: And he left the linen cloth, and fled from them naked (14:50–52).
>
> And entering into the sepulchre, they saw a young man sitting on the right side, clothed in a long white garment (16:5b).

The mysterious character of the young man functions as the spirit or angel in each of these two very different situations found in chapters 14 and 16 respectively.[4] The old worldly way is evident in the young man's first appearance at Jesus's arrest. At that time, Jesus was abandoned by all and overcome by violent, worldly force. The spirit of the event was fear and disorder, and so the young man fled, naked and vulnerable. In his later appearance in the tomb, the young man is no longer naked but "clothed in a long white garment"; he is no longer running away in panic but "sitting on the right side" (5), calmly informing the women of Jesus's

---

4. Similar to the spirits or angels that personify the corporate character of each of the seven churches that Christ addresses in the book of Revelation, the young man represents the character or nature of each of the two situations in which he appears, showing again the great contrast between the old and the new.

Taking In and Giving Out (Mark 16)

resurrection. The spirit of the new situation is now "right," and the young man speaks as only an angel or benevolent supernatural messenger could: he tells the women Jesus is risen, instructs them of his whereabouts, and where the disciples are to find him in Galilee; he even knows that Jesus has already told them as much (7).

THE WOMEN'S RESPONSE

Verse 8, the final verse of the first half of Mark's sixteenth chapter, describes the impact the new has upon the women: they are amazed and fearful, and so they tell no one of their encounter.

It is the women's reaction that evokes a recollection of my own inward experience and, in part, allows me to interpret this narrative, for my response to my first encounter with the transcendent presence of Christ was as theirs. Amazed at the unanticipated dimension of existence, I was nevertheless convinced of its truth, as the epiphany was irrefutable. Like the women in this story, I felt constrained to tell no one of it; nor did I, for more than a year: my old suppositions and reasoning were so utterly upended by my new experience that I needed time to integrate all parts of my life into a new understanding that was coherent; responsive to God; and dwelt, at last, in peace. It took time for the radical metaphysical shift to settle in my mind and heart, and I was prevented from revealing my inward state until I felt sufficient stability to withstand whatever the world in its confusion and contrariness would cast in my direction, for I knew its nature as a refugee knows her escaped country.

PART TWO (9-20): RECIPROCALITY

As the first half of this chapter was about *taking in* the new reality of resurrection, the second half is about *giving out* one's testimony to that resurrection; that is, it is about the telling and presenting to others the new reality that has formed within oneself. The coherence in chapter 16 is provided through the dynamic of reciprocality: the "taking in" and the "giving out" of the gospel, for the text is arranged to teach the reader this first axiom of the new and living way. Once the gospel is received (the first half), it must be ministered to the world (the second half). It cannot be stated too strongly that it is inappropriate to attempt to force a literal interpretation or scholarly explanation upon the seeming vagaries of this text.[5]

The second half of the chapter begins by referring to the power himself: "Now when Jesus was risen early the first day of the week,[6] he appeared first to Mary Magdalene" (9). Unlike Mary's response in the first half of the chapter, in the second half, she "went and told them that had been with him" (10). For from verse 9 on, the focus is no longer upon taking in the new but upon giving or revealing it to others. Mary appears in both the first and second halves, not to show continuity in the plot (in fact, her appearance shows the discontinuity!) but to stand as an example or prototype of the individual who first receives and then transmits the gospel to others. That it is a woman who is the first to minister the gospel underscores the need—first of all—for inward receptivity.[7] In that she tells the men who are in a weakened state of mourning and weeping for what has passed (10), she carries the message of the power of God that heals the broken-hearted; resurrects to life; and imbues and fills with power, even "the weaker vessel," as the most prominent disciple among them has designated her sex to be (1 Pet 3:7).

---

5. Verses 9–20 are present in 99 percent of manuscripts, yet two codices from the fourth century end with verse 8 (Sinaiticus and Vaticanus). Earlier in the late second century, Irenaeus had quoted Mark 16:19 in *Against Heresies* (Book III, Chapter 10), indicating the passage's composition preceded its omission.

6. Again, we see the newness conveyed by the words "early the first day of the week."

7. That Jesus "cast seven devils" from Mary Magdalene is interpreted to mean (1) that spiritual restoration is required to minister the gospel, and (2) that the severity of the initial inward state matters not; everyone can be restored. In fact, it is only those who are aware of the need to be healed who are, in fact, those who are prepared to be healed, as Jesus ironically tells the scribes and Pharisees earlier: "They that are whole have no need of the physician, but they that are sick: I came not to call the righteous, but sinners to repentance" (2:17).

Taking In and Giving Out (Mark 16)

LESSON ON RECEPTIVITY (11-14)

Are all as receptive to the gospel as Mary Magdalene was in the second half of this chapter? Verses 11 through 14 answer this question and thus prepare ministers who routinely will encounter lack of receptivity in those to whom they witness. "And they, when they had heard that he was alive, and had been seen of her, believed not" (11). The lesson ministers are to learn before beginning their work is that there will be a lack of receptivity on the part of those who hear their witness. No minister should see this as a personal failure, for lack of receptivity typically occurs whenever the gospel is preached, a fact conveyed in this passage by the repetition of yet another example of unbelief (12). Jesus appears to two disciples, who, like Mary, tell the others of their encounter, and again the remainder of the disciples are unreceptive: "neither believed they them" (13). Only after Jesus appears directly to the eleven is there an intimation the remaining disciples have believed; that is to say, there's no further mention of their "unbelief." What in this passage is certain, however, is that the responsibility for unbelief is squarely placed on the hearers and not upon the ministers of the gospel. The minister must learn that most will not receive the testimony of "them which had seen him after he was risen" (within themselves), and they must continue their work undeterred by that reaction. Jesus assigns responsibility for this lack when he pronounces judgment and upbraids the unreceptive for "hardness of heart" (14).

COMMISSION AND SIGNS (15-18)

Having been warned of the lack of receptivity that awaits them, the disciples/ministers are then commissioned to go out to "preach the gospel": to *give out* the Word, everywhere, far and wide (15). Once again, they are reminded of this essential fact: a lack of acceptance faults the hearer, not the speaker: "He that believeth and is baptized shall be saved; but he that believeth not shall be damned" (16). The stakes are high: it is the salvation of the world through the transformation—the convincement/conviction—of each person in it.

Verses 17 and 18 list signs that indicate belief has occurred: that is to say, that the ministered gospel, the knowledge of God, has been received and taken in. Those who have taken in, that is, been transformed by the inward knowledge of God will be given power that is indicated by certain signs. In Christ's power, "name," they shall "cast out devils," i.e., rid their own and others' souls of foundational, existential error (17). They will know and "speak with new tongues," i.e., they will be given to speak/minister the Word of God, who is Christ (17). They shall be able to withstand worldly, demonic (serpent-like) assault without incurring harm to their souls, even though, unwittingly, they have taken in the venom, as though having drunk "a deadly thing" (18). And at their hand, the spiritually sick and debilitated will be restored to life (18). An attempt to interpret literally verses 17 and 18 indicates that belief has not yet occurred.

RECIPROCALITY IN HEAVEN

The final two verses of this chapter complete the theme of reciprocality: the taking in and the giving forth of the gospel. After the Lord had instructed the disciples of the particulars of their mission (15–18), he is "received up into heaven, and sat on the right hand of God." Just as earlier, the young man also sat "on the right side" (5) and gave the women information about Jesus, Jesus as Lord now sits at God's "right hand" and gives forth his Substance, the gospel power. To whom is he giving his Light and Word? With whom does he work throughout time from within eternity? The final verse of Mark's Gospel answers our questions and sends us forth:

> And they went forth, and preached every where, the Lord working with them, and confirming the word with signs following. Amen.

Bibliography

Barclay, Robert. *Apology for the True Christian Divinity.* Glenside, PA: Quaker Heritage, 2002.
Dallmann, Patricia. *Abiding Quaker* (blog). patradallmann.com.
Fox, George. *The Works of George Fox.* Philadelphia: Marcus C. Gould, 1831.
Gates, Tom. "George Fox and the Bible: A Dual Legacy." *Friends Journal* (2024). https://www.friendsjournal.org/george-fox-and-the-bible/
Glines, Elsa F. ed. *Undaunted Zeal: The Letters of Margaret Fell.* Richmond, IN: Friends United, 1974. Hirsch, Frank E. "Abomination of Desolation." In The International Standard Bible Encyclopaedia, 1:16. Grand Rapids: Eerdmans, 1939.
Jacobs, Alan. *The Year of Our Lord 1943: Christian Humanism in an Age of Crisis.* Oxford: Oxford University Press, 2018.
La Grange du Toit, Philip, and Iver Larsen. "Olivet Discourse." Wikipedia. https://en.wikipedia.org/wiki/Olivet_Discourse.
Molinos, Miguel, Jeanne-Marie Guyon, and Francois Fenelon. *A Guide to True Peace*, facsimile of 1815 edition compiled by William Backhouse and James Janson. Sebastopol, CA: Jim Wilson, 2019.
Nayler, James. *The Works of James Nayler.* Farmington, ME: Quaker Heritage, 2003–2009.
Nickalls, John L., ed. *The Journal of George Fox.* London: London Yearly Meeting of the Religious Society of Friends, 1985.
Ohio Yearly Meeting (Conservative). *Book of Discipline of Ohio Yearly Meeting of the Religious Society of Friends.* Barnesville, Ohio: Yearly Meeting, 2022. https://ohioyearlymeeting.org/wp-content/uploads/2023/12/Advices.pdf.
Orr, James. "Herodians." In T*he International Standard Bible Encyclopaedia*, 3:1383. Grand Rapids: Eerdmans, 1939.
Penington, Isaac. *The Works of Isaac Penington.* Glenside, PA: Quaker Heritage, 1995–1997.
Penn, William. *No Cross, No Crown.* Wadsworth, OH: Friends Library, 2021.
Pink Floyd. "Another Brick in the Wall," on the album *The Wall.* Columbia P2T36183, 1979, cassette.

BIBLIOGRAPHY

Raskin, Jamie. *Unthinkable: Trauma, Truth, and the Trials of American Democracy.* New York: Harper, 2022.

Russell, Bertrand. "Bertrand Russell's Nobel Prize Acceptance Speech." Reason and Meaning. https://reasonandmeaning.com/2015/10/08/bertrand-russells-nobel-prize-acceptance-speech/#google_vignette

Smith, William T. "Number." In *The International Standard Bible Encyclopaedia,* 4:2159, 2162. Grand Rapids: Eerdmans, 1939.

Thomson, J.E.H. "Sadducees." In *The International Standard Bible Encyclopaedia,* 4:2660. Grand Rapids: Eerdmans, 1939.

———. "Pharisees." In *The International Standard Bible Encyclopaedia,* 4:2365. Grand Rapids: Eerdmans, 1939.

Union for Reform Judaism. "Kavod Hameit." ReformJudaism.Org., 2025. https://reformjudaism.org/glossary/kavod-hameit.

Wallace, T.H.S., ed. *None Were So Clear.* Camp Hill, PA: New Foundation, 1996.

Weems, Anne B. *Psalms of Lament,* "Jesus Wept." Richard Rohr Daily Meditation in Center for Action and Contemplation. https://cac.org/daily-meditations/jesus-wept-2023-04-18/.

"Why the Lack of Religion Breeds Mental Illness." Academy of Ideas. https://academyofideas.com/2022/05/why-the-lack-of-religion-breeds-mental-illness/.

Williams, Charles B. "Tradition." In *The International Standard Bible Encyclopaedia,* 5:3004. Grand Rapids: Eerdmans, 1939.

www.ingramcontent.com/pod-product-compliance
Lightning Source LLC
Chambersburg PA
CBHW071214160426
43196CB00012B/2298